DISABILITY AND THE DISABLED-ISSUES

WORK AND PLAY FOR THE DISABLED: RESEARCH ON INCREASED PARTICIPATION

DISABILITY AND THE DISABLED-ISSUES

Additional books in this series can be found on Nova's website under the Series tab.

Additional E-books in this series can be found on Nova's website under the E-book tab.

LAWS AND PROGRAMS

Additional books in this series can be found on Nova's website under the Series tab.

Additional E-books in this series can be found on Nova's website under the E-book tab.

DISABILITY AND THE DISABLED-ISSUES

WORK AND PLAY FOR THE DISABLED: RESEARCH ON INCREASED PARTICIPATION

LAUREN S. RANDOW
EDITOR

Nova Science Publishers, Inc.
New York

LIBRARY OF CONGRESS CATALOGING-IN-PUBLICATION DATA

Work and play for the disabled: research on increased participation /
editor, Lauren S. Randow.
p. cm.
Includes index.
ISBN 978-1-61122-463-4 (hbk.)
1. People with disabilities--Employment--United States. 2. People with disabilities--Recreation--United States. I. Randow, Lauren S.
HD7256.U5W68 2010
331.5'9--dc22

2010037375

Published by Nova Science Publishers, Inc. ✝ New York

CONTENTS

PREFACE

The reasons why workers with disabilities continue to face the possibility of losing their jobs or being unable to return to the workforce are many and complex. In addition to challenges resulting directly from their health conditions, individuals may have trouble obtaining employment services such as job counseling or training to help them stay in their current job or find a new one. Limited access to health care or other financial supports may also make it challenging for individuals to manage their disabilities and maintain their connection to the workforce. Additionally, improving work participation for individuals with disabilities can be challenging because, beyond individuals themselves, numerous stakeholders play an important role in the process. This book examines the current research on actions that could increase work participation for adults with disabilities.

Chapter 1- The Americans with Disabilities Act (ADA)—now in its 20th year—calls for the full participation of individuals with disabilities in society, including the workforce. Yet, many barriers exist that may prevent them from staying connected or returning to employment. For instance, eligibility requirements for receiving public disability benefits or health coverage are not always consistent with helping to keep individuals at work or facilitating their return. Also, employers may not know how to accommodate employees with disabilities or may lack financial incentives to do so.

GAO convened a forum on March 16, 2010, to explore policy options and actions that could be taken to help adults with a current or past work history improve their participation in the workforce. Participants included experts and officials representing a variety of views. Prior to the forum, GAO surveyed a larger group of experts to help inform the discussion. Comments expressed during the forum or on the survey do not necessarily represent the views of all participants, the organizations they represent, or GAO.

Although GAO is not making recommendations, based on the authors prior work and consistent with a past GAO proposal to Congress, GAO agrees with forum participants that strong federal leadership is essential for achieving the level of coordination required to effectively leverage resources to improve work participation for Americans with disabilities.

Chapter 2- Research has established that physical activity and participation in athletics provides important health and social benefits for children. Certain federal laws help ensure that kindergarten-12th grade schools provide students with disabilities opportunities to participate in physical education (PE) and extracurricular athletics equal to those of their peers. However, national associations have questioned whether students with disabilities receive opportunities similar to their peers.

Regarding students with disabilities, GAO was asked to examine (1) what is known about the PE opportunities that schools provide, and how do schools provide these; (2) what is known about the extracurricular athletic opportunities that schools provide, and how do schools provide these; and (3) how the Department of Education (Education) assists states and schools in these areas. GAO analyzed federal survey data; reviewed relevant federal laws and regulations; and interviewed state, district, and school officials in selected states, as well as parents and disability association officials.

In: Work and Play for the Disabled: Research on... ISBN: 978-1-61122-463-4
Editor: Lauren S. Randow

Chapter 1

ACTIONS THAT COULD INCREASE WORK PARTICIPATION FOR ADULTS WITH DISABILITIES

United States Government Accountability Office

WHY GAO CONVENED THIS FORUM

The Americans with Disabilities Act (ADA)—now in its 20th year—calls for the full participation of individuals with disabilities in society, including the workforce. Yet, many barriers exist that may prevent them from staying connected or returning to employment. For instance, eligibility requirements for receiving public disability benefits or health coverage are not always consistent with helping to keep individuals at work or facilitating their return. Also, employers may not know how to accommodate employees with disabilities or may lack financial incentives to do so.

GAO convened a forum on March 16, 2010, to explore policy options and actions that could be taken to help adults with a current or past work history improve their participation in the workforce. Participants included experts and officials representing a variety of views. Prior to the forum, GAO surveyed a larger group of experts to help inform the discussion. Comments expressed during the forum or on the survey do not necessarily represent the views of all participants, the organizations they represent, or GAO.

Although GAO is not making recommendations, based on our prior work and consistent with a past GAO proposal to Congress, GAO agrees with forum participants that strong federal leadership is essential for achieving the level of coordination required to effectively leverage resources to improve work participation for Americans with disabilities.

What Participants Said

From the policy options identified through two surveys and discussions at a 1-day forum, participants prioritized the following actions for improving work outcomes at three levels: individual, employer, and federal.

Individual: Participants articulated a key underlying principle for increasing work participation—improve incentives for individuals with disabilities to work while strengthening necessary services and supports. Participants generally agreed that a more coordinated system of programs and benefits is needed to encourage individuals to work and remove the structural barriers that can jeopardize the services and supports they depend on. They also noted that an increased emphasis on benefits counselors could be useful in helping individuals coordinate the services they receive. However, participants cautioned that any new approaches should be structured to avoid unintended consequences, such as adversely affecting those who cannot work or have yet to enter the workforce.

Employer: Participants focused on two proposed actions to further engage and encourage employers in helping individuals with disabilities keep their jobs or return to work. The first involved creating a well-structured information campaign to educate employers about the benefits of keeping employees with disabilities at work or helping them return to work. This campaign would include information about the financial benefits of retaining these employees, as well as narratives from companies who have been successful in doing so. Participants emphasized the importance of disseminating information through a variety of media outlets and involving the disability and business communities in the process of developing the campaign. The second action involved enhancing incentives for employers to keep or return individuals to work by increasing their responsibility for some of the long-term costs of disability. This could be done either by requiring employers to directly finance extended disability benefits for their employees or by adjusting employers' payroll taxes based on their success at keeping employees in the workforce. Ideally, both actions would motivate employers to increase their use of services and practices that proactively address potentially disabling conditions and reintroduce individuals to the workplace.

Federal: To address the actions proposed above, or other broad policy options, participants agreed that a federal coordinating entity is needed to focus and align efforts across numerous federal agencies and programs that play a role in supporting individuals with disabilities. They noted that to be effective, interagency efforts would need strong support from the White House; and to ensure legitimacy, a coordinating entity would need representation from the disability community. Participants also suggested that the federal government could do more to serve as a model employer of individuals with disabilities and that more research is needed on hiring practices and retention levels of individuals with disabilities within the federal workforce.

ABBREVIATIONS

ADA	Americans with Disabilities Act
ACS	American Community Survey
RTW	return-to-work
SAW	stay-at-work
SSA	Social Security Administration
SSDI	Social Security Disability Insurance
SSI	Social Security Income
Ticket to Work Program	Ticket to Work and Self-Sufficiency Program
VR	Vocational Rehabilitation
VR&E	Vocational Rehabilitation and Education
WIA	Workforce Investment Act
WIPA	Work Incentives Planning and Assistance

INTRODUCTION

This year marks the 20th anniversary of the Americans with Disabilities Act of 1990 (ADA)—a landmark piece of civil rights legislation that promotes access and opportunity for millions of Americans with disabilities and calls for their full participation in society, including in the workforce. Nevertheless, despite the promises and hope ignited by the ADA, parity in workforce participation for Americans with disabilities has remained elusive. Most telling, the unemployment rate of individuals with disabilities seeking work remains well above those without disabilities, and the gap has widened further in recent years.[1]

The reasons why workers with disabilities continue to face the possibility of losing their jobs or being unable to return to the workforce are many and complex. In addition to challenges resulting directly from their health conditions, individuals may have trouble obtaining employment services such as job counseling or training to help them stay in their current job or find a new one. Limited access to health care or other financial supports may also make it challenging for individuals to manage their disabilities and maintain their connection to the workforce. Additionally, improving work participation for individuals with disabilities can be challenging because, beyond individuals themselves, numerous stakeholders—including employers, health care providers and various federal, state, and local programs—play an important role in the process. Each of these stakeholder groups may either lack information relevant to their role—such as recommended actions for helping the individual stay employed and the costs and benefits of those actions—or may lack financial incentives to take on that role.

The complexity of these and other challenges related to improving work participation is a major reason why GAO placed modernizing federal disability programs on its high-risk list in 2003.[2] Progress toward greater work participation has remained difficult in part because the United States has a patchwork of disability programs—developed individually over many years—but lacks a unified set of national goals that guide coordination among programs or contribute to measuring desired outcomes. Specifically, our past work has identified 20 federal agencies and almost 200 programs that provide a wide range of assistance—including employment-related services—to people with disabilities.[3] Given this disarray in disability programs, we have proposed that Congress take the lead in authorizing a coordinating entity to develop a federal strategy that could integrate services and support;[4] however, we also recognize that leadership is not the sole purview of Congress and that the executive branch must also help lead the way. Strong leadership is even more necessary at a time of economic downturn and constrained government budgets.

Within this context, we convened a 1-day forum on March 16, 2010, to identify public and private sector options for, and the federal government's role in, assisting adults with disabilities in their efforts to remain employed or return to the workforce. To ensure that we focused on the most important issues, prior to the forum we iteratively surveyed 60 individuals with subject matter or professional expertise to solicit input and help determine the forum's agenda. Of the 60 survey recipients, 17 were invited to participate in our 1-day forum. Forum participants included federal officials, researchers, disability advocates, and medical and vocational service providers, among others, and as a whole reflected a wide array of sectors, professions, and perspectives.[5] Informed by the survey results, and with the help of consensus and facilitation techniques, forum participants fleshed out issues related to providing incentives, services, and cash and health benefits to individuals, and proposed actions related to improving education, tools, and incentives to employers.[6] They also discussed the federal government's role in implementing their proposals and other policies to support individuals with disabilities. This report summarizes key options and issues identified through the forum discussion and surveys we conducted. See appendix I for more information on our process for selecting survey respondents, forum participants and policy areas; appendix IV for the forum agenda; and appendix V for a list of forum participants.

The perspectives expressed herein do not necessarily represent the views of all participants, the organizations they represent, or GAO. We thank all of the participants for the generous contribution of their time and constructive exchange of views and ideas during the forum and within the survey responses. This report is available at no charge and in accessible format on GAO's Web site at http://www.gao.gov.

Daniel Bertoni

Daniel Bertoni, Director
Education, Workforce, and Income Security Issues
July 29, 2010

BACKGROUND

Evidence Suggests Many Individuals with Disabilities Can and Want to Work

Data suggest that many individuals with disabilities—including some who are currently unemployed—can and want to work. Recent Census data estimated that 40 percent of working-age individuals[7] who reported having a disability were employed.[8] At the same time, many experts believe that these employment figures fall short of the number of individuals with disabilities who could participate in the workforce. For example, according to 2008 Census data, an estimated 9 percent of unemployed individuals with disabilities between the ages of 21 and 64 in 2008 were actively looking for work.[9] Also, analysis conducted by Mathematica Policy Research, Inc. found that 40 percent of working-age Social Security Administration (SSA) disability benefit recipients reported having goals of work or saw themselves working in the future.[10]

Current thinking and research suggest that mitigating workplace barriers would help individuals with disabilities to stay employed. Broadly defined and for the purposes of this report, a disability is the existence of a health condition that impedes an individual's ability to function in his or her environment, either temporarily or for a prolonged period. According to the Institute of Medicine, the World Health Organization and others, a disability is not just the existence of a health condition, but an interaction of that health condition with barriers created by the individual's physical and social environments.[11] While some health conditions may be too severe to allow for continued employment, research shows that with appropriate and tailored supports—such as a wheelchair, a flexible work schedule or text-reading software—some individuals with disabilities can successfully function in the work environment.[12] Current concepts of disability also suggest that perceptions held by employers and physicians and the individuals themselves may create unnecessarily low expectations about individuals' abilities to participate in the workforce, and can affect whether an individual finds or retains employment.

Furthermore, the timing of interventions has an effect on whether an individual with a health condition can stay in or return to the workforce. Current research demonstrates the importance of providing employment services and medical benefits soon after the onset of disability. For example, the American College of Occupational and Environmental Medicine recommends that individuals at risk for leaving the workforce due to disability coordinate early and closely with their health care provider, employer and insurer, to address medical and environmental needs.[13] Experts note that the longer an individual is out of the workforce, the more difficult it is to return.[14]

Private and Public Disability Insurance and Income Support Programs

Private disability insurance programs can provide timely cash benefits to individuals with disabilities, although many individuals are not covered by these programs. Private disability insurance coverage, sometimes subsidized by employers, is designed to partially replace lost income when an individual is unable to work due to a disability.[15] To help manage the costs of providing these cash benefits, private employers and insurers may also provide a variety of work supports to individuals to help them stay at or return to work. In 2009, approximately one-third of employees in the private sector and state or local government had access to some form of disability insurance through their employers.[16]

Additionally, all states have workers' compensation programs which provide partial salary replacement and pay medical expenses for employees who sustain work-related injuries and illnesses.[17] Workers' compensation programs also provide other services to help injured and ill workers stay at or return to work. Employers pay the cost of premiums for workers' compensation programs or may self-insure. Employers' premiums (or direct costs if they are self-insured) are generally determined by the number of claims paid to their employees. This creates incentives for providing safe work environments and retaining individuals after injury or illness.

Generally viewed as a resource of "last resort," the Social Security Administration (SSA) provides income support to some individuals with disabilities through the Social Security Disability Insurance (SSDI) and Supplemental Security Income (SSI) programs.[18] Beneficiaries of these programs can also qualify for Medicare or Medicaid health insurance. To be eligible for SSDI and SSI benefits due to disability, individuals must have a physical or mental impairment that prohibits them from engaging in work constituting "substantial gainful activity."[19] Concerns have been raised that SSA program rules for receiving benefits—such as tying the definition of substantial gainful activity to income thresholds—can create incentives to stay out of the workforce, even when work is possible. Similarly, SSI beneficiaries lose their entitlement to Medicaid benefits when their earnings reach a certain threshold for a period of time. To protect health care eligibility, some beneficiaries may decline to seek or choose to limit employment.[20] In part to improve work incentives and work participation for SSA's disability beneficiaries, Congress passed the Ticket to Work and Work Incentives Improvement Act of 1999, which among other provisions, created the Ticket to Work and Self-Sufficiency Program (Ticket to Work Program).[21] Although intended in part to improve access to and expand the availability of work-related supports,[22] the Ticket to Work Program experienced early disappointing results in terms of the extent that individuals and service providers participated in the program.[23] Consequently, SSA revised the Ticket to Work Program regulations in 2008 to encourage greater participation by service providers;[24] however, the impact of these changes has yet to be determined.

Federal Employment Services for Individuals with Disabilities

A variety of federal programs are designed to provide services to individuals with disabilities to improve work participation. The Department of Education's (Education) Vocational Rehabilitation (VR) programs, Veterans Affairs' Vocational Rehabilitation and Education (VR&E) program, and the Department of Labor's Workforce Investment Act (WIA) One-Stop Career Centers all provide services that assist individuals in finding or retaining employment. Beyond these programs aimed at providing one-on-one assistance to individuals, the Department of Labor's Office of Disability Employment Policy (ODEP) provides myriad education and assistance to employers and communities, as well as individuals, related to increasing work participation of individuals with disabilities.

While these programs provide important services, their scope and structures pose some challenges for improving work participation, including coordination among agencies. Specifically, individuals in need of assistance may not always have access to or receive timely or appropriate services. For example, resource limitations within Education's VR program can lead to eligible individuals being placed on waitlists if they are not among those with the most significant disabilities.[25] See table 1 for a description of key services and supports available to individuals with disabilities as well as challenges they present to keeping or finding employment.

Table 1. Key Services and Supports Available to Adults with Disabilities, and Their Limitations

Programs or offices	Description	Limitations
Private and public disability insurance and income support programs		
Private disability insurance	Provides partial income repla-cement for policy holders who are unable to work due to disability.	Not all individuals have disability insurance.
State short-term disability insurance	Select states require the provi-sion of time-limited partial income replacement for indivi-duals who are unable to work due to disability.	Only applies to indivi-duals in five states.
State workers' compensation	Provides partial income repla-cement and medical coverage for individuals who sustain work-related injuries or illness.	Provides supports only for individuals whose disabilities are job-related.
Social Security Disability Insurance (SSDI)	Provides cash benefits to qual-ifying individuals with a physical or mental impairment that prevents them from working for at least one year.	Five month waiting period to collect benefits is not conducive to helping individuals remain in the workforce; bene-fits stop if individual earns above an income threshold which may occur before financial independence can be achieved.
Social Security Supplemental Security Income (SSI)	Provides cash benefits to individuals with disabilities who have low income or resources and who meet the same medical eligibility requirements as for SSDI.	Like SSDI, benefits stop if earnings are above an income threshold, but SSI has more grad-ual benefit reductions that are more supportiveof return to work.

Table 1. (Continued)

Programs or offices	Description	Limitations
Federal medical benefits		
Health and Human Services Medicare program	Provides health care coverage to seniors and some indivi-duals with disabilities; SSDI recipients are eligible to receive benefits.	For those under 65 applying for benefits because of disability, there is a 24-month waiting period before benefits start, which is not conducive to helping individuals remain in the workforce.
Health and Human Services Medicaid program	State-administered medical assistance provided to individuals with disabilities who meet state-designated eligibility criteria, including having income and assets below certain thresholds.	Benefits stop if individual exceeds an income or asset threshold, which may occur before financial independence can be achieved.
Federal programs that provide employment services		
Department of EducationVocationalRehabilitation programs	Employs counselors to help individuals achieve employment goals; provides tailored services such as job placement and training, medical treatment, and assistive technology.	Resource limitations can prevent some individuals from receiving timely services.
Department of Veterans Affairs' Vocational Rehabilitation and Employment program	Provides individualized services to address the employment-related barriers of veterans with a service-connected disability.	The program may lack flexibility to address some barriers.
Department of Labor's Workforce Investment Act (WIA) One Stop Career Centers	Provides employment assistance, including to individuals with disabilities. Some centers have disability program navigators—staff who provide support to other WIA staff serving individuals with disabilities and who work to improve links to employers.	Funding for the disability program navigators ended after federal fiscal year 2009, and concerns exist about individuals' with disabilities access to WIA services.

Table 1. (Continued)

Programs or offices	Description	Limitations
Department of Labor's Office of Disability Employment Policy	Provides a variety of resources and services to individuals, employers and community organizations to increase employment for individuals with disabilities.	Many resourcesprovid-ed are demonstration projects that have yet to be fully implemented.
Social Security Administration's Ticket to Work Program	Provides a ticket to SSDI and SSI beneficiaries to receive employment services from approved private or public providers of employment services.	Early results regarding participation in the program by individuals and service providers were disappointing and the effect of recent changes to the program has yet to be determined.

Source: Review of literature and prior GAO work.

Beyond these major programs, numerous federal programs provide a variety of assistance to individuals with disabilities, which may in turn affect work outcomes. For example, our prior work found that, in the federal sector alone, there are nearly 200 programs under 20 agencies that provide services or supports to people with disabilities.[26] Given the multiple dimensions of disability and the variety of relevant private and public programs, many stakeholders may be involved in the process of keeping or returning an individual to work.

Focus on the Individual: Improve Incentives and Strengthen Existing Services and Supports

Participants articulated a guiding principle that policy options should improve incentives for individuals with disabilities to work while strengthening the supports and services on which they depend. In particular, they noted that individuals have a variety of basic needs that must be met, such as income, housing, health care, and access to transportation. As such, individuals with disabilities or their representatives generally respond rationally to the incentives or disincentives presented to them when considering whether working or not is the best way to meet these needs. Participants stated that as programs and benefits are currently structured, it often does not pay to work because individuals are only able to receive the income, housing, and/or other supports and services they need if they do not work or limit their earnings. Incentives need to be aligned so that work becomes the rational choice for individuals who can work and not the risky choice.

Participants identified four key components of this principle to help ensure policy options effectively improve incentives and workforce participation for individuals with disabilities:

1. *Provide a coordinated system of supports and services that make it possible to work and still have basic needs met.* Current federal disability programs are structured such that they may place individuals in situations where working is unattractive. For instance, panelists said that SSDI beneficiaries may be hesitant to return to the workforce if their wages will eventually disqualify them from continuing to receive Medicare health benefits and if they believe they will be denied or not offered coverage by a prospective employer. Some individuals returning to work can receive Medicaid coverage through the Medicaid Buy-in Program.[27] However, one participant noted that this program may inadvertently keep individuals in poverty because states place limits on the amount of income or resources the individual can have and maintain eligibility for Medicaid. Given the variety of programs and stakeholders involved in providing supports and services, the task of creating an improved and coordinated system is a difficult one. For example, this could involve taking inventory of existing benefits and programs to see where gaps in coverage exist, where coordination would improve delivery of services, and how programs could be aligned and refined to improve incentives.
2. *Create earlier opportunities to access services and benefits.* Participants stated that policies should allow individuals to receive a broad array of supports and services before a disability forces them to leave the workforce. Currently, many individuals lack private disability insurance,[28] so they may not have access to services and benefits until after they have left the workforce. For instance, individuals must leave the workforce for a period of time and prove they are unable to engage in substantial employment because of a physical or mental impairment before they can start to receive SSDI and Medicare benefits. In general, participants noted that interventions are needed well before this point to provide options for

individuals to stay in the workforce and reduce the need for Social Security benefits. Such interventions could include partial disability benefits that take effect when an individual cannot work full-time. To be timely and more effective, participants suggested that any new interventions should have more flexible eligibility criteria and provide for earlier access to a wider set of supports and services than those currently offered through Social Security programs.

3. *Tailor services and supports to the needs of individuals, e.g., using benefits counselors.* In addition to emphasizing that services and supports should be tailored to individual needs, participants suggested that enhanced benefits counseling would help individuals make informed decisions and better choose personalized supports and services in response to work opportunities. Benefits counseling could also help make individuals aware of the options available to them and help coordinate the various services they may receive in relationship to their individual needs. One participant noted that even in the absence of new incentives, the information provided by benefits counselors could help improve work participation for adults with disabilities by helping to address some of the fears individuals may have about returning to work.[29]
4. *Evaluate the costs and benefits of new interventions.* Participants stated that the cost and benefits of new services and benefits will need to be demonstrated through research and evaluation. However, the costs and benefits of new initiatives may be difficult to evaluate given the various programs and stakeholders involved. For example, a new program that may lower costs for SSA may increase costs for other agencies or organizations. Therefore, costs and benefits should be evaluated at a level that takes this into consideration rather than in terms of individual programs.

Participants cautioned that any new services or benefits need to be structured carefully to avoid creating any unintended negative consequences. Interactions between benefit eligibility requirements and earnings need to be understood to avoid scenarios where individuals might return to work only to lose an existing benefit—such as subsidized housing—before employment is truly sustainable. Additionally, new efforts should not be implemented at the expense of needed supports and services for individuals with serious, long-term disabilities who cannot work, such as many of those receiving SSDI. For instance, one participant noted that if Social Security were to provide short-term disability benefits, these benefits should be complementary to and not jeopardize entitlement to SSDI for those who rely on this basic income.

In addition to the guiding principle and key components discussed, forum participants, as well as survey respondents, identified additional actions related to improving incentives for individuals that may warrant further exploration. Examples include the following actions:

- *Enhance tax incentives for individuals to work.* The federal government should explore the possibility of a disabled worker earned income tax credit as a way to help individuals cover the additional costs of disability and help them remain employed.[30]
- *Modify the Family and Medical Leave Act of 1993.*[31] The law could be modified to improve individuals' ability to return to their former employers. This could be done by allowing individuals who are no longer working for an employer because they exhausted their medical leave to apply for open positions with that former employer as internal (versus outside) candidates.
- *Promote and facilitate a team approach to helping individuals stay at work or return to work.* Several forum participants and survey respondents noted the importance of prompt coordination and communication among stakeholders at the onset of a disability, including with the individual with the disability, family members, employer, health care providers, employment services providers, and others.

FOCUS ON THE EMPLOYER: IMPROVE KNOWLEDGE AND INCENTIVES

Recognizing the essential role that employers must play in improving work participation for individuals with disabilities, two groups of participants proposed actions to increase employers' efforts to help individuals with disabilities keep working or return after an absence. One group proposed actions for increasing employers' knowledge about the financial benefits of retaining or rehiring employees with disabilities. Another group of participants proposed actions for improving financial incentives for employers by increasing their share in the costs resulting from employees leaving the workforce because of disability. In both cases, participants said that while these actions could increase employment for people with disabilities and decrease their use of public disability benefits such as SSDI, significant challenges and issues exist that would need to be addressed with input from employers when designing and implementing these actions.

Develop an Information Campaign to Improve Employers' Knowledge about the Financial Benefits of Retaining Individuals with Disabilities or Returning Them to Work

One group of participants proposed developing an information campaign to improve employers' knowledge about the financial benefits of retaining employees with disabilities or returning them to work. Participants noted that most efforts to increase retention and rehiring to date have focused on employers' legal responsibilities rather than the financial advantages possible for businesses. Retaining individuals after the onset of disability could decrease staff turnover costs and allow employers to retain those with important skills, abilities, and institutional knowledge, according to participants. Also, individuals with disabilities can represent to employers a large market of potential customers, and employees with disabilities can provide important perspectives on attracting these customers.

Participants said the information campaign should incorporate both new and existing research on the financial benefits of retaining or rehiring employees after the onset of disability.[32] They stressed the importance of conducting up-to-date research tailored to specific industries and focused on employers' needs. For example, the research could compare the average cost of providing accommodations versus the costs of hiring and training a replacement employee. In addition to providing quantitative cost savings information, the information campaign should include descriptive examples of effective practices used by employers and the financial benefits realized. These examples should include a diverse array of employer sizes and types of disabilities. They could also illustrate how employers' efforts to prevent and accommodate disabilities—such as using flexible work environments—can positively impact the workforce as a whole.

The support and participation of both the business and disability communities would be crucial to the campaign's success. Participants stated that businesses would be more likely to embrace the campaign if it were produced by a well-known private sector research entity[33] rather than a federal agency or non-profit organization tasked with increasing employment of individuals with disabilities. The campaign could initially focus on a few industries likely to grow in the coming decades, with the possibility of expanding the campaign to additional industries if it proved successful.

Participants emphasized the importance of distributing information on financial benefits through a strategic and coordinated marketing campaign. To ensure the message reaches different types of employers, the campaign should disseminate information through new forms of media like Internet social networking; more traditional media like major newspapers and business publications; as well as business-to-business networks and communication. The environmental sustainability movement was also identified as a potentially useful model for marketing the information. In particular, participants suggested adopting the environmental movement's strategy of involving high-profile business executives to enhance acceptance within the business community.

A successful information campaign would have economic and social benefits, according to participants. Such a campaign could convince employers to retain or rehire employees with disabilities in higher numbers, and decrease reliance on public benefits. If better informed, employers may show an increased commitment to supporting individuals with disabilities and employees may feel more comfortable and confident disclosing their disabilities. Ultimately, high-performing employees with disabilities could provide positive examples for employers and further increase their commitment to supporting other individuals with disabilities.[34]

Participants also identified some potential limitations and challenges to improving employment through an information campaign. These included the following:

- *An information campaign alone might not be enough to improve work outcomes.* Participants debated how effective an education campaign would be without also changing incentives for individuals and employers. One participant noted that employers are good at calculating financial benefits and therefore may already be acting in the most cost-effective manner, given current incentives. However, another participant noted that existing cultural biases against individuals with disabilities may lead employers to make retention and hiring decisions based on misperceptions rather than economic facts.

- *The information campaign could increase overall retention and hiring but have limited success for individuals with certain disabilities.* Some participants expressed concern that misconceptions about certain types of disabilities might persist, leading employers to limit retention and hiring of individuals with those disabilities. They suggested that this could be partially addressed by including illustrative examples that focused on the contributions of employees with various types of disabilities. Participants also acknowledged that some individuals with disabilities may have conditions that are too severe to make work feasible.
- *Past information campaigns have had limited success.* Participants noted that there have been past government efforts toeducate employers on the financial benefits of employing individuals with disabilities, but they did not improve employment outcomes to desired levels. Therefore, the entity designing the information campaign should identify and implement the lessons learned from previous efforts. For example, improved marketing strategies for disseminating this information might lead to better outcomes than past efforts.
- *Government programs that provide resources to employers would need to be prepared for increased demand.* If the information campaign convinced employers to retain or hire more individuals with disabilities, employers would likely increase their use of federal programs that support work. Government programs such as the VR program would need to be better publicized and their services enhanced to support employers' expanded interest and efforts. Making these improvements may require additional program funding.

Enhance Employer Incentives to Mitigate Work Disabilities by Increasing Their Financial Responsibility for Employees Who Exit the Workforce

Another group of participants concluded that because employers generally do not directly bear the long-term costs associated with their workers' disabilities not covered by workers' compensation programs, they have little financial incentive to provide benefits and services to retain employees after the onset of disability.[35] Accordingly, these participants proposed two approaches that would increase employers' costs when their employees leave the workforce due to disability. In view of the fact that the proposed approaches allow employers to control the costs by keeping employees at work, participants thought that employers would therefore have added incentives to adopt timely and effective intervention strategies to keep employees working.

- *Adjust payroll taxes according to an employer's success at keeping employees in the workforce*: This approach would modify the payroll tax structure used to fund the SSDI program. Unlike the current approach wherein payroll tax rates are the same for all employers, rates would be adjusted so that employers who are successful at keeping their employees with disabilities at work would pay less than those with many employees leaving the workforce and entering the SSDI program. Participants referenced state workers' compensation and unemployment insurance programs as examples of how this "experience rating" approach can improve employers' incentives.[36]
- *Require employers to provide disability benefits*:[37] Employers would be required to finance disability benefits for an extended period of time if employees' disabilities prevented them from performing job duties.[38] Participants suggested that many employers would fulfill their financial responsibilities by purchasing private disability insurance plans. Employers' financial responsibilities for providing benefits could be partially subsidized by the federal government. For example, subsidies could be paid for by diverting some revenues from existing payroll taxes.

Participants anticipated that either approach would motivate employers to more quickly support individuals with disabilities and keep them at work in order to minimize the costs of providing cash benefits. Employers could do this through a variety of practices such as providing accommodations, working with employees to identify safe and appropriate work tasks, or modifying company policies to make it easier for employees to return to work after short absences. It could also involve creating a company culture where the expected course of action after the onset of a disability is to take steps that promote continued work rather than immediate retirement. Participants noted that improved employer practices could also benefit workers without disabilities by increasing employers' support of employee wellness programs.

Successful efforts to keep more people at work would also have financial benefits for the federal government, according to participants. For example, while there would be a continuing need for SSDI to provide cash benefits for individuals with severe long-term disabilities,[39] improved employer practices could decrease the number of individuals applying for and relying on SSDI benefits, and increase the number of workers paying taxes. Participants also anticipated a decreased need for SSDI employment and work incentive programs, since the individuals who would most likely participate in these programs would earlier receive employment services to keep them working. As such, some funds could be redirected from Ticket to Work and other work incentive programs to efforts to address disabilities earlier by federal employment programs.

While expressing hope for the success of these approaches, participants identified key challenges that would need to be addressed, including the following:

- *Avoid creating incentives for employers to not hire job applicants they believe to be at greater risk of work disability.* Participants acknowledged that this would be an important issue to resolve in designing an employer-incentive system. They thought this challenge could be partially mitigated by their proposals to subsidize employers' disability-related expenses and to increase services provided by federal employment programs to individuals who are still employed. In addition, participants noted that new and existing tax credits to reward employers who hire individuals with disabilities could minimize this challenge. This concern might also diminish over time because employers would start to consider the costs associated with addressing disabilities as a standard part of doing business.
- *Privacy concerns about increased employer involvement in managing employee health.* Employer practices to support employees with disabilities could increase their access to employees' health information—a situation which may make employees uncomfortable. One participant stated that this concern could be minimized by medical providers working with individuals to explain to the employer what the individual can and cannot do, rather than providing medical information about the disability itself.
- *Establishing experience-rated payroll taxes for small businesses.* It could be difficult to accurately experience rate payroll taxes for small employers due to their relatively low number of employees. Determining payroll tax rates based on some method of risk pooling—such as by using the experiences of business sectors rather

than individual businesses—could partially address this challenge. However, risk pooling has limitations because individual employers' behavior would not have a direct impact on their tax rate. Research on the experiences of private sector workers compensation and disability insurance rating could provide additional options for structuring experience-rated tax rates for small businesses.

Participants suggested that further research or demonstrations would be important to identify strategies to mitigate these and any unforeseen challenges (such as a disproportionate burden on specific industries); identify the impact on demand for other federal programs; and determine cost-effectiveness. Pilot programs and demonstration projects focused on one business sector could also test the incentive design, gain employer perspective, and allow for exploration of alternative approaches.

Additional Options for Improving Incentives, Education, and Tools for Employers, Insurers, and Service Providers

In addition to the two proposals identified and discussed during the forum, participants and survey respondents identified additional actions to improve incentives, education, and tools for employers, insurers and various service providers, such as providers of medical and vocational rehabilitation. Examples include the following actions:

Incentives

- *Expand tax incentives for employers to retain and hire individuals with disabilities.* One survey respondent suggested increasing Work Opportunity Tax Credit reimbursement rates and another suggested creating financial incentives for federal contractors to hire people with disabilities.[40] Tax incentives could also be used to reimburse employers for providing accommodations.
- *Develop a "Ticket to Stay At Work" program for employers or insurers.* Employers or private insurers could receive payment for successful efforts to retain employees who might otherwise enter the SSDI program.[41]

- *Modify publicly funded health insurance programs to better compensate health care providers for disability management.* Potential modifications include altering Medicaid fee schedules to compensate medical professionals for consultations and actions aimed at keeping or returning an individual to work.
- *Partially offset employers' health care costs for individuals with disabilities to improve incentives for retention and hiring.* Public health care programs could cover some of the health care costs incurred by employers of those with disabilities.

Education and Tools

- *Improve education and ongoing training for health care providers and employment service providers.* Several participants and survey respondents stated that many health care providers are too quick to recommend that individuals leave the workforce after the onset of disability. Medical school and continuing education curriculums could include more information about medical providers' roles in identifying ways for individuals to stay employed or quickly return to work.[42] Similarly, participants recommended developing additional degree programs and continuing education curriculum for employment service providers.
- *Improve the process for disseminating education and tools to employers and service providers.* Existing education and tools could be better leveraged if employers and service providers could access them all from one central clearinghouse. Participants suggested that this clearinghouse would be most effective if it could be accessed in a variety of ways, not just via the Internet.

FOCUS ON THE FEDERAL GOVERNMENT: COORDINATE EFFORTS AND SERVE AS A MODEL EMPLOYER

To help design and implement their proposals and other options for improving work participation, participants suggested that the federal government create a coordinating entity to help focus and align efforts across agencies. A major obstacle to implementing comprehensive, successful, and timely interventions is that responsibility for crucial supports and services is spread across various agencies. For example, a participant noted that disability insurance is administered by SSA, while the Departments of Education, Labor, and Health and Human Services administer services to help individuals return to work. A coordinating entity could help tie together existing funding streams and resources and use them in new ways. This suggestion is consistent with past GAO work that suggested Congress create a coordinating body to develop strategies for integrating services and supports for individuals with disabilities.[43] Both GAO and a participant noted that a past entity—the National Coordinating Council for Disabilities—was formed but never convened, representing a lost opportunity to coordinate efforts.

Additionally, one participant suggested an interagency demonstration project as another way to foster collaboration between agencies and test options for improving work outcomes. For example, several agencies could be charged with developing a pilot program to address a specific proposal—such as increasing employers' incentives to retain workers—as a way to test the effectiveness of the proposal and determine how to best work together.

The right organizational structure and strong executive leadership is needed in order for agency collaborations to succeed. Participants noted that past interagency efforts have not been very successful at achieving significant change because they have lacked sufficient authority, accountability, or resources. One participant commented that, as a member of many interagency working groups, she has seen useful ideas go unused because no one agency took ownership for the ideas or the staff involved were not empowered to take the actions needed to implement them. Another participant noted that although his agency has a data-sharing agreement with a second agency, he must implement the agreement in his spare time because neither agency has devoted sufficient resources to the effort. Several participants emphasized that the impetus for coordination needs to come from the White House because federal agencies will be responsive when the White House identifies an initiative as a priority and holds agencies accountable for its success. One participant suggested that the White House could set a clear goal for employment of individuals with disabilities and hold agencies accountable for meeting it. He felt that without this strong push from above, agencies would emulate past efforts and fail to make meaningful changes.

Successful interagency efforts should also have strong buy-in from a variety of stakeholders. One participant noted that stakeholders from the disability community and private sector need to come together to agree on new efforts. Another participant agreed and added that it would be useful to obtain consensus from disability advocates on the key barriers that individuals with disabilities face in finding and keeping employment and how existing programs contribute to these barriers.

In addition to better coordinating disability programs, participants felt that the federal government could do more to be a model employer of individuals with disabilities. Several participants agreed that it would seem inappropriate for the federal government to ask others to improve their employment of individuals with disabilities if its own track record is lacking. Participants noted some recent federal efforts aimed at improving employment for people with disabilities, such as an executive order[44] issued by the President to encourage the employment of veterans—including those with disabilities—and a governmentwide hiring fair for individuals with disabilities. However, participants said that existing special authorities to expedite the hiring of individuals[45] are not well understood by many agencies. Additionally a participant noted that programs intended to support hiring of individuals in the federal government can be complex. The participant suggested that the federal government could inventory the programs and efforts available to improve employment outcomes for individuals with disabilities and do a better job of advertising them.

A participant noted that steps could be taken to reassess the workers' compensation program for federal workers. According to this individual, the Federal Employees' Compensation Act provides generous benefits and gives injured workers little incentive to return to work. He noted that injured workers can receive benefits equivalent to as much as 75 percent of their wages tax-free and can continue to receive benefits as long as their condition persists, sometimes past retirement age. These conditions provide a powerful disincentive for returning to work, as most workers would be financially better off collecting benefits.

One participant also suggested that the federal government could improve its disability management practices by conducting research on why employees with disabilities leave the federal workforce. For example, although the federal government captures self-reported disability information from employees at the time they are hired, it may not be updated after this point. Therefore, researchers have little information about federal employees who leave the workforce due to disabilities incurred after they become employed.

CONCLUDING OBSERVATIONS

Our forum participants and survey respondents identified specific issues and actions that they felt needed to be addressed and taken that would improve employment for individuals with disabilities. Clearly, actions recommended for increasing work participation need to be considered in light of economic and fiscal constraints. As the economy struggles to recover from conditions that have produced business downturns and high unemployment, policy considerations such as those aimed at increasing work participation of individuals with disabilities need to take into account the overall costs and benefits to employers. Similarly, as the federal government faces mounting financial constraints, and the costs and benefits of public programs face greater scrutiny, initiating additional actions may seem daunting. At the same time, these overarching considerations provide compelling motivation for advocates, business, and government leaders to consider alternatives and work together to address the existing fragmented program structure, reduce program inefficiencies, improve the seamless provision of information and services, and ultimately increase work participation for Americans with disabilities who want to work.

To this end, our prior work and forum participants agree that strong federal leadership—from both Congress and the Executive Branch—coupled with appropriate organizational structures and stakeholder input, is essential for achieving the level of coordination and cooperation required to make the best use of resources and increase work participation. GAO has articulated this concern on numerous occasions and highlighted it by including federal disability programs on our high-risk list for the past 7 years. Similarly, we agree it would be difficult to convince private employers to increase their employment of individuals with disabilities without the federal government improving its own employment practices and taking the lead as a model employer.

APPENDIX I. SCOPE AND METHODOLOGY

To identify options for improving work participation for adults with disabilities, we solicited the views of a wide range of experts through a series of surveys and through a forum comprised of a subset of survey respondents.

The forum as a whole was designed to reflect a wide array of sectors, professions, and perspectives.

Identifying and Prioritizing Options for Improving Work Outcomes

To gather opinions from experts about how to improve work participation for individuals with disabilities and help determine the agenda of our forum, we employed a modified version of the Delphi method. The Delphi method follows a structured process for collecting and distilling knowledge from a group of experts by means of a series of questionnaires. For our purposes, we employed two iterative electronic surveys.

Our first survey was comprised of open-ended questions and asked respondents to provide their views on the strengths and weaknesses of current approaches in terms of keeping adults with disabilities at work or returning them to work, as well as suggestions for improving current approaches and federal policies. We sent this survey to 60 individuals and received completed surveys from 50 respondents, for a response rate of 83 percent. See appendix II for a copy of the first Delphi survey.

The first survey was conducted between December 2009 and January 2010, using a self-administered electronic survey. We sent the survey by e-mail in an attached Microsoft Word form that respondents could return electronically after entering responses into open-answer boxes. We sent out reminder email messages and made several courtesy phone calls to nonrespondents to encourage a higher response rate.

Based on the 50 completed surveys, we performed a content analysis of the open-ended responses related to suggestions for improving current approaches and federal policy, and ultimately categorized these suggestions into 10 broad topic areas. The second survey was conducted between February and March 2010. In our second survey, we asked recipients to rate each topic area (on a scale of 1 through 5) in terms of their importance for improving work participation for adults with disabilities. In addition, we asked respondents to identify and rank in order the three topics they considered most important for improving work participation. We sent this survey to the same 60 individuals and organizations and received completed surveys from 45 for a response rate of 75 percent. See appendix III for a copy of the second Delphi survey.

Because these two surveys were not sample surveys, but rather surveys of the universe of respondents we identified, they have no sampling errors. However, the practical difficulties of conducting any survey may introduce errors, commonly referred to as nonsampling errors. For example, difficulties in interpreting a particular question, differences in sources of information available to respondents, or differences when entering data into a database or analyzing them can introduce unwanted variability into the survey results. We took steps in developing the surveys, collecting the data, and analyzing them to minimize such nonsampling errors. For example, GAO design methodologists designed the surveys in conjunction with GAO staff who had subject matter expertise. Additionally, we conducted a series of pretests with several survey recipients prior to distributing both surveys. The goals of the pretests were to ensure that (1) the questions were clear and unambiguous and (2) terminology was used correctly. We made changes to the content and format of both surveys as necessary during the pretesting processes.

Using the rankings participants assigned to our topics in the second survey, we developed a weighted score for each topic by assigning a respondent's top choice three points, the second choice two points, and the third choice one point. Table 2 shows the relative ranking of our 10 topics.

On the day of the forum, we provided survey results to the subset of survey recipients who were selected as forum participants. At the beginning of the forum, we asked our participants to consider the survey results and, with the help of trained GAO facilitators, reach consensus on three topics that would be the focus of the day's discussions. Our participants ultimately decided to consolidate the top seven ranked topics to form three broader topics to focus on during the forum, as follows:

1. providing incentives and supports to individuals;
2. providing education and tools to employers, insurers, and service providers; and
3. improving incentives for employers, and insurers and service providers.

Table 2. Rank Ordering of Survey Respondents' Most Important Policy Options

Policy option		Number of respondentsindicating option among topthree in importance:			Weighted Score
		1st	2nd	3rd	
1.	Enhance incentives for employers, insurers, health care providers and private sector service providers to increase the participation in, and supportfor, stay-at-work (SAW) and return-to-work (RTW) efforts.	10	8	12	58
2	Increase health insurance access and coverage provisions for individuals who are candidates for SAW and RTW.	8	7	4	42
3.	Enhance and reconcile income support systems through one or more of the following: modifying disability benefit rules, creating partial or temporary benefits, or revising current laws or regulations guiding income supports.	6	8	6	40
4.	Increase education and provide tools for employers and public and private sector service providers to assist in increasing work participation for persons with disabilities.	10	2	3	37
5.	Enhance incentives for individuals to engage in SAW and RTW efforts.	4	6	5	29
6.	Expand access to individualized SAW and RTW services and supports.	3	5	7	26
7	Provide training and education to health care professionals about the benefits and attributes of successful SAW and RTW interventions.	4	6	2	26
8.	Increase coordination and collabor-ation between state, federal, and private sector stakeholders.	0	2	3	7
9.	Enhance research on issues related to SAW and RTW.	0	1	3	5
10.	Increase consumer access to information about SAW and RTW resources and laws.	0	0	0	0

Source: GAO.

Note: We asked survey respondents to indicate their top three choices in terms of topics to discuss at the forum. The weighted scores in this figure were calculated using the following points: Rank of 1st (3 points); 2nd (2 points), 3rd (1 point). Forty-five respondents completed this survey.

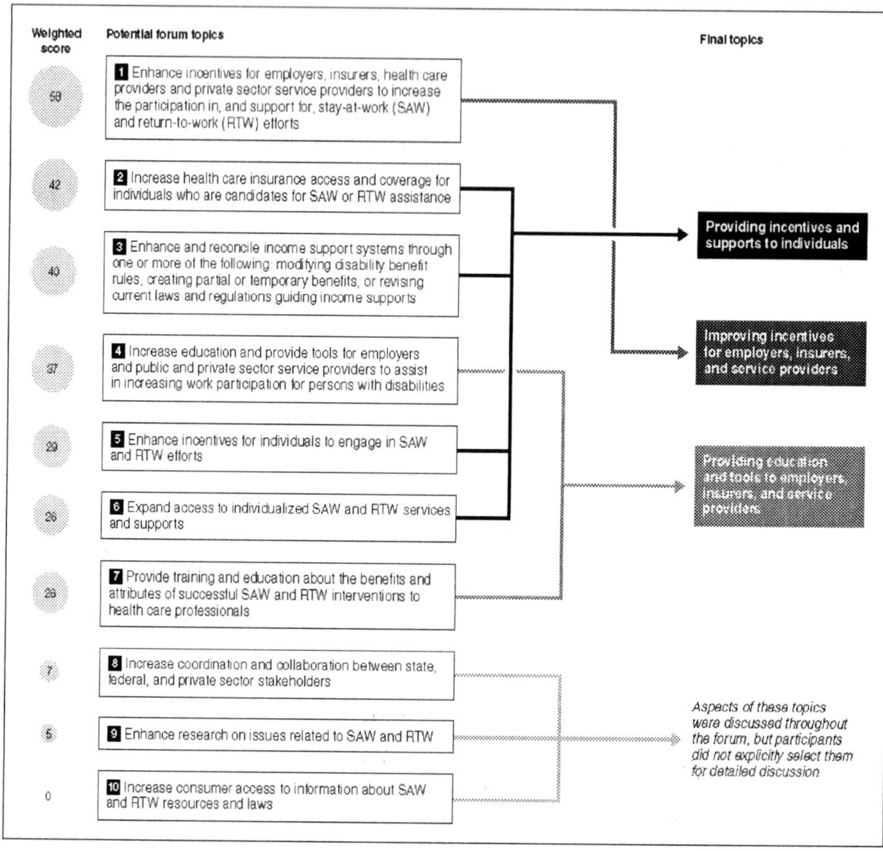

Source: GAO.

Figure 1. Forum Participants Narrowed Down Policy Topics from 10 to 3

After participants decided on these topics, GAO facilitators helped participants form three subgroups. During breakout sessions, each subgroup was responsible for focusing on one topic and coming to consensus on one proposed action for improving work participation for individuals with disabilities. Participants in the first subgroup that focused on providing incentives and supports to individuals discussed key issues but did not have sufficient time to reach consensus on a proposed action. Participants in the second and third subgroups discussed options for providing or improving education, tools and incentives for insurers and service providers, but ultimately proposed actions that focused on employers. After the breakout session, the subgroups reconvened to present their proposals to the full group and solicit input. Lastly, the forum participants discussed how the federal government could support and foster their proposals. For a copy of the forum agenda, see appendix IV.

Selecting Survey Recipients

We used a three-step process to determine the individuals and organizations who would be invited to participate in our Delphi surveys. First, we identified professional sectors (both public and private) that have a stake and/or expertise in retaining individuals with disabilities at work or in helping them return to work. Based on our literature review, interviews with experts, and consultation with internal experts we identified the following sectors:

1. federal agencies and commissions;
2. private disability insurance companies;
3. employers;
4. organizations representing people with disabilities;
5. medical providers;
6. researchers;
7. state benefits and employment support programs; and
8. other employment supports (including community-based, private, etc.).

Next, within each of these sectors, we identified key organizations and individuals. Our decisions were informed by the following:

- recommendations we received from external and GAO experts on disability;
- membership in the National Academy of Social Insurance;
- authorship of key research; and
- professional credentials.

As a final determining factor, leveraging internal subject matter expertise, we sought to achieve balance with respect to individuals' professional perspective, professional background, geographic location, and knowledge of policy proposals and demonstration projects.

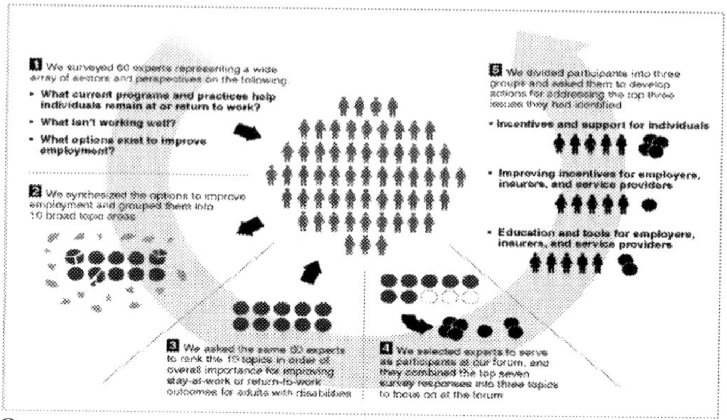

Source: GAO.

Figure 2. Process for Choosing Forum Topics

To help ensure that our selection was thorough, we asked respondents in our first survey to recommend additional groups or individuals who they felt should be included. Additional groups or individuals identified through this process were invited to complete both surveys based on the criteria described above.

Selecting Participants

We selected a subset of survey recipients to participate in our 1-day forum. We initially planned to convene a forum of 12 to 16 participants—a number we considered appropriate to allow full participation by each participant and be manageable from a logistics standpoint.[46] Beyond this, our selection was based on the following considerations:

- The forum should include representatives from key federal agencies and at least one representative from each of the stakeholder categories used in identifying questionnaire respondents;
- each participant should bring a sufficiently broad perspective on stay-at-work or return-to-work (based on their professional experience, position, and/or publications); and
- taken together, the forum would reflect a variety of perspectives and experiences regarding policy development and evaluation.

See appendix V for a list of forum participants. The following chart summarizes our process for selecting participants and topics.

APPENDIX II. FIRST DELPHI SURVEY

United States Government Accountability Office

GAO
Accountability * Integrity * Reliability

Survey About Intervention Strategies to Help Adults with Disabilities Stay at Work or Return to Work

Introduction

Many disability policy experts agree that interventions designed to assist adults with work-related disabilities in staying at or returning to work can increase their participation in work and society, and decrease reliance on public benefits. At the same time, uninsured individuals may not have access to stay-at-work or return-to-work services when most needed, and gaps and limitations exist with respect to publicly available stay-at-work or return-to-work services. Through an iterative survey process and a live forum, GAO hopes to explore and identify: essential components of successful intervention strategies; areas of agreement or disagreement about the strengths and weaknesses of current public and private sector programs and practices; the costs, benefits and challenges of promising policy options for improving existing or providing new services (including financing options); and next steps for federal, state, and private stakeholders.

To accomplish this goal, we need your help. The purpose of this survey is to ask a range of informed experts and practitioners, like yourself, to identify key elements and issues regarding promising interventions that help adults with impairments or disabilities stay at work or return to work. This is the first of two surveys. A second survey will be sent to the same experts and practitioners asking them to rate the importance of issues identified in this survey. Following, GAO will convene a subset of respondents at a live forum in Spring 2010 to discuss key strategies and policy options identified through this process in more detail. In the end, we plan to issue a product that summarizes the results of the questionnaires and forum, without direct attribution to any specific participant.

The focus of these surveys and forum is limited to interventions for adults who experience a disability after already having an attachment to the workforce. We refer to ***stay-at-work*** interventions as those designed to help individuals who have a connection to the workforce stay at work, even if they are currently on medical leave. We refer to ***return-to-work*** interventions as those designed to assist individuals who no longer have a connection to the workforce.

Instructions for Completing this Survey

This survey will take about 30-45 minutes to complete. To complete the survey, first save this document to your computer. You may then enter your responses directly to that file. All of the questions are open-ended. To respond, just place your cursor in the response area and start typing. You may enter as much text as you wish since the boxes will expand to accommodate your answers.

When you have completed this survey, please attach the document to an e-mail and send to us at EarlyIntervention@gao.gov. Because of our very ambitious timeline, we ask that you **please submit your response no later than December 23, 2009**. If you have any questions, please contact Daniel Concepcion at 312-220-7688 or Barbara Steel-Lowney at 415-904-2172. You may also email us at EarlyIntervention@gao.gov.

Thank you for your participation!

Contact Information

Please enter your contact information below so we can follow-up with you if necessary.

Name:

Title:

Organization:

Telephone Number:

Email Address:

Section A: Successful Strategies for Stay-at-Work or Return-to-Work Interventions

Based on previous work, a range of experts and professionals working in disability-related areas identified four strategies as key to developing a framework for stay-at-work and return-to-work interventions:[1]

1. Intervene (with medical and employment supports, etc.) as soon as possible after an actual or potentially disabling event to promote and facilitate stay-at-work or return-to-work outcomes.
2. Identify and provide necessary stay-at-work or return-to-work assistance that is tailored to an individual's needs and goals.
3. Provide coordination services to assist individuals in navigating programs and achieving their stay-at-work or return-to-work goals.
4. Structure incentives, including cash and medical benefits, to encourage stay-at-work or return-to-work behaviors.

1. What changes or additions, if any, would you make to these four strategies in terms of achieving successful stay-at-work interventions?

2. What changes or additions, if any, would you make to these four strategies in terms of achieving successful return-to-work interventions?

[1] These four strategies are based on GAO's current work and *SSA Disability: Return-to-Work Strategies from Other Systems may Improve Federal Programs*. GAO/HEHS-96-13.

Section B: Strengths of Current Approaches

3. What elements in existing public and private sector programs are you aware of that contribute to helping individuals with disabilities stay at work?

4. What elements in existing public and private sector programs are you aware of that contribute to helping individuals with disabilities return to work?

Section C: Weaknesses or Gaps in Current Approaches

5. What shortcomings or gaps in existing public and private sector programs are you aware of that may deter individuals from staying at work?

6. What shortcomings or gaps in existing public and private sector programs are you aware of that may deter individuals from returning to work?

Section D: Options for Improving Current Approaches

7. Given the strengths and weaknesses you identified regarding existing stay-at-work efforts, what changes do you think need to take place to improve outcomes and who should implement these changes?

8. Given the strengths and weaknesses you identified regarding existing return-to-work efforts, what changes do you think need to take place to improve outcomes and who should implement these changes?

Section E: Potential Improvements in Federal Policy

9. What do you see as the two or three most important steps the federal government can take to improve or promote stay-at-work interventions?

10. What do you see as the two or three most important steps the federal government can take to improve or promote return-to-work interventions?

Section F: Recommendations for Participants in our Efforts

11. To ensure we reach all appropriate stakeholders, please identify individuals or organizations you think should participate in this questionnaire. We will endeavor to send the questionnaire to those not already contacted, time permitting.

APPENDIX III. SECOND DELPHI SURVEY

United States Government Accountability Office

GAO
Accountability • Integrity • Reliability

Intervention Strategies to Help Adults with Disabilities Stay at Work or Return to Work

Second Questionnaire

Introduction

Thank you for participating in the survey we sent out earlier. Based on your input, we were able to identify a range of key elements and issues regarding interventions that help adults with impairments or disabilities stay at work (SAW) or return to work (RTW). We synthesized the suggestions you and others provided, to create this second survey on possible discussion topics to cover when we convene a forum of experts in March 2010.

This questionnaire is asking you, along with the same experts and practitioners who participated in the first survey, to rate the importance of issues identified in the previous survey. Because we have limited time during our one-day forum to discuss these complex topics, the purpose of this second survey is to identify the topics you believe are most important in terms of improving outcomes for adults with a prior work history.

Information from both surveys will be presented in aggregate and summary form without attribution to specific individuals.

Instructions

For each discussion topic, we ask that you first rate the overall importance of each item and then rank the <u>three most important topics that you feel should be addressed at the forum and highlighted in our report to Congress.</u>

This questionnaire should take less than 15 minutes to complete. To complete the survey, first save the MS Word file containing the questionnaire to your computer. You may then enter your responses directly to that file. You can simply click on the response boxes to select or deselect your answer ☒.

When your questionnaire has been completed, save your responses and send the file as an e-mail attachment to us at <u>EarlyIntervention@gao.gov</u>.

To have your input considered by the forum, please submit your response **<u>by February 12, 2010</u>.** Please contact Daniel Concepcion at 312-220-7688 regarding any questions on completing the survey or its content. Alternately, you may contact Barbara Steel-Lowney at 415-904-2172, or email us at <u>EarlyIntervention@gao.gov</u>.

Section 1: Rating of Policy Options

Below are broad policy options we synthesized from responses to our first survey. Each option may encompass a number of more specific options or actions, which will be discussed at our forum. Please rate the following policy options as to their overall importance for improving stay-at-work and/or return-to-work outcomes for adults with disabilities.

Policy Options	No importance ▼	Little importance ▼	Moderate importance ▼	Much importance ▼	Extreme importance ▼
1. Increase education and provide tools for employers and public and private sector service providers to assist in increasing work participation for persons with disabilities.	☐	☐	☐	☐	☐
2. Increase consumer access to information about SAW and RTW resources and laws.	☐	☐	☐	☐	☐
3. Provide training and education to health care professionals about the benefits and attributes of successful SAW and RTW interventions.	☐	☐	☐	☐	☐
4. Expand access to individualized SAW and RTW services and supports.	☐	☐	☐	☐	☐
5. Enhance research on issues related to SAW and RTW.	☐	☐	☐	☐	☐
6. Enhance incentives for employers, insurers, health care providers and private sector service providers to increase the participation in, and support for, SAW and RTW efforts.	☐	☐	☐	☐	☐
7. Enhance incentives for individuals to engage in SAW and RTW efforts.	☐	☐	☐	☐	☐

Policy Options	No importance	Little importance	Moderate importance	Much importance	Extreme importance
8. Increase health insurance access and coverage provisions for individuals who are candidates for SAW and RTW.	☐	☐	☐	☐	☐
9. Increase coordination and collaboration between state, federal and private sector stakeholders.	☐	☐	☐	☐	☐
10. Enhance and reconcile income support systems through one or more of the following: modifying disability benefit rules, creating partial or temporary benefits, or revising current laws or regulations guiding income supports.	☐	☐	☐	☐	☐

Section 2: Rank Ordering for Most Important Policy Options

Of the ten policy options listed above, which one do you feel is the most important, second most important, and third most important?

1. **Most Important:** **Click and select ...**
2. **Second Most Important:** **Click and select ...**
3. **Third Most Important:** **Click and select ...**

Section 3: Key Policy Research Studies

If you are aware of key research studies related to any of your top three policy options listed above that you feel should be shared with the panel, please list them below.

APPENDIX IV. FORUM AGENDA

GAO
Accountability * Integrity * Reliability

Forum

Improving Work Outcomes for Adults with Disabilities
March 16, 2010
Staats Briefing Room, 7C13

8:00-8:30 Registration and Morning Refreshments

8:30-9:00 Opening Session

Welcome & Introductions

- Barbara Bovbjerg—Managing Director, Education, Workforce and Income Security

Setting the Stage

- Daniel Bertoni—Director, Education, Workforce and Income Security
- Patricia Owens—Senior Level Expert, Disability Programs and Issues

9:00-9:45 Identify Key Policy Areas Affecting Work Outcomes
In response to two pre-forum surveys, 60 experts identified, rated and ranked key policy areas that affect work outcomes for adults with disabilities. Informed by these results, panelists will come to consensus on three key policy areas to discuss during the forum.

Moderators:

- Patricia Owens—Senior Level Expert, Disability Programs and Issues
- Andrew Stavisky— Senior Design Methodologist, Center for Design, Methods, and Analysis

9:45-10:00 Break

10:00-11:45 Break-out Sessions to Identify and Discuss Actions for Key Policy Areas

Panelists will break into three groups, each focusing on one of the three key policy areas. Each group will discuss possible actions within its assigned policy area, and related stakeholders, benefits, challenges and cost-effectiveness.

Moderators:

- Daniel Bertoni—Director, Education, Workforce and Income Security
- Patricia Owens—Senior Level Expert, Disability Programs and Issues
- Michele Grgich—Assistant Director, Education, Workforce and Income Security
- Andrew Stavisky— Senior Design Methodologist, Center for Design, Methods, and Analysis
- Terry Richardson— Senior Design Methodologist, Center for Design, Methods, and Analysis
- Cindy Saunders— Senior Design Methodologist, Center for Design, Methods, and Analysis

11:45-12:00 Break

12:00-1:00 Legislative Priorities and Opportunities

A panel of staff from relevant congressional committees will discuss legislative priorities and opportunities and respond to expert panelists' questions to inform their deliberations. Lunch will be served.

Moderators:

- Daniel Bertoni—Director, Education, Workforce and Income Security
- Terry Richardson— Senior Design Methodologist, Center for Design, Methods, and Analysis

1:00-2:30 Full Group Discussion of Actions Identified During Breakout Sessions

Panelists will report on the results of the morning break out sessions. All panelists will have an opportunity to ask questions and provide input.

Moderators:

- Patricia Owens—Senior Level Expert, Disability Programs and Issues
- Andrew Stavisky— Senior Design Methodologist, Center for Design, Methods, and Analysis
- Terry Richardson— Senior Design Methodologist, Center for Design, Methods, and Analysis

2:30-2:45	**Break**
2:45-3:45	**Next Steps: Federal Role in Supporting and Implementing Potential Actions** *Panelists will discuss the federal role in supporting and implementing actions identified and defined in earlier sessions.* Moderators: o Daniel Bertoni—Director, Education, Workforce and Income Security o Patricia Owens—Senior Level Expert, Disability Programs and Issues o Andrew Stavisky— Senior Design Methodologist, Center for Design, Methods, and Analysis o Terry Richardson— Senior Design Methodologist, Center for Design, Methods, and Analysis
3:45-4:00	**Wrap-up** Moderators: o Daniel Bertoni—Director, Education, Workforce and Income Security

APPENDIX V. FORUM PARTICIPANTS

Gerald B. Bacon	Assistant Director of Rehabilitation Services—Vocational Rehabilitation and Employment, Department of Veterans Affairs
Richard Balkus	Associate Commissioner—Program Development and Research, Social Security Administration
Richard V. Burkhauser	Professor—Departments of Economics and Policy Analysis & Management, Cornell University
Marianne Cloeren	Board Member and Fellow—American College of Occupational and Environmental Medicine; Medical Director—Managed Care Advisors, Inc.
Marty Ford	Director of Legal Advocacy—The Arc and UCP Disability Policy Collaboration
Janet Fiore	Chief Executive Officer—The Sierra Group
Howard H. Goldman	Professor of Psychiatry—University of Maryland School of Medicine
Gary Goosman	Director—TOWER Initiative, US Business Leadership Network

(Continued)

Shelby Hallmark	Director—Office of Workers' Compensation Programs, Department of Labor
Andrew J. Imparato	President and Chief Executive Officer—American Association of People with Disabilities
Helen Lamont	Long-Term Care Policy Analyst—Office of Disability, Aging, and Long-Term Care Policy, Office of the Assistant Secretary for Planning and Evaluation, Department of Health and Human Services
Nancy Magee	Vice President—Disability Benefits Operations, Unum Life Insurance Company of America
Rita Martin	Deputy Director—Council of State Administrators of Vocational Rehabilitation
Joe Razes	Senior Technical Advisor—Centers for Medicare and Medicaid Services
Colonel James S. Rice	Director—U.S. Army Wounded Warrior Program
LynnaeRuttledge	Commissioner—Rehabilitation Services Administration, Department of Education
David Stapleton	Senior Fellow and Director—Center for Studying Disability Policy, Mathematica Policy Research Inc.

Source: GAO.

BIBLIOGRAPHY AND RESOURCES

The following citations provide a sampling of publications and information that we selected with respect to general disability policy and the three topic areas selected by forum participants. In some cases, citations will be listed under more than one topic area.

General Work Disability Policy

[1] American College of Occupational and Environmental Medicine. (2006). "Preventing Needless Work Disability by Helping People Stay Employed." Elk Grove Village, Ill..

[2] Brandt, Edward N. Jr. & Andrew M. Pope, eds. (1997). *Enabling America: Assessing the Role of Rehabilitation Science and Engineering.*

Institute of Medicine of the National Academies. Washington, D.C.: National Academy Press.

[3] Berkowitz, Edward. (1987). Disabled Policy: America's Programs for the Handicapped-A Twentieth Century Fund Report. New York and London: Cambridge University Press.

[4] Christian, Jennifer, et al. (2009). *Introduction to the New Work Disability Prevention Paradigm.* Wayland, Mass.,60 Summits Project, Inc..

[5] Field, Marilyn J. & Alan M. Jette, eds. (2007). *The Future of Disability in America.* Institute of Medicine of the National Academies. Washington, D.C.: National Academies Press.

[6] Jette, Alan. (2006). "Toward a Common Language for Function, Disability, and Health." *Physical Therapy*, vol. *86*, no. 5. 726-734.

[7] Mashaw, Jerry L. & Virginia P. Reno, eds. (1996). *Balancing Security and Opportunity: The Challenge of Disability Income Policy.* Washington, D.C.: Disability Policy Panel, National Academy of Social Insurance.

[8] Mashaw, Jerry L., Virginia P. Reno, Richard V. Burkhauser& Monroe Berkowitz, eds (1996). *Disability, Work and Cash Benefits.* Kalamazoo, Mich.: W.E. Upjohn Institute for Employment Research.

[9] National Council on Disability. (2009). *National Disability Policy: A Progress Report.* Washington, D.C..

[10] Organisation for Economic Co-Operation and Development. (2006, 2007, 2008). *Sickness, Disability and Work: Breaking the Barriers*, vols. 1-3 (France).

[11] Department of Labor Office of Disability Employment Policy. (2010). *A New Day: We're Listening Webcasts.* Washington D.C., 2010. http://www.dol.gov/odep/disabilitylistening.htm (accessed on June 15).

Providing Incentives and Supports to Individuals

[1] American College of Occupational and Environmental Medicine Special Committee on Health, Productivity and Disability Management. (2009). "Healthy Workforce/Healthy Economy: The Role of Health, Productivity, and Disability Management in Addressing the Nation's Health Care Crisis." *Journal of Occupational and Environmental Medicine,* vol. *51*, no.1: 114-119.

[2] American College of Occupational & Environmental Medicine and Integrated Benefits Institute. (2008). *Improving the Health and Productivity of the American Workforce: A Blueprint for Action. Consensus Statements and Recommendations from the First National Workforce Health and Productivity Summit*. Santa Ana Pueblo, New Mexico.

[3] Andrews, Kristin, Bob Weathers & Su Liu.(2007). "How Do Medicaid Buy-In Participants Who Collect Social Security Disability Insurance Benefits Use SSA Work Incentive Programs?" *Mathematica Policy Research, Inc. Working with Disability Work and Insurance in Brief*, no. 7. Princeton, N.J., December.

[4] Brown, Randall, Carol Irvin, Debra Lipson, Sam Simon & Audra Wenzlow. (2008). *Research Design Report for the Evaluation of the Money Follows the Person (MFP) Grant ProgramFinal Report.* Mathematica Policy Research, Inc. Prepared for the Centers for Medicare and Medicaid Services.Princeton, N.J., October.

[5] Consortium for Citizens with Disabilities. (2008). *Statement of Principles: Social Security Disability Program Work Incentives and Related Issues*. Washington, D.C., January

[6] Consortium for Citizens with Disabilities. *Independence, Empowerment & Security. (2008). The Consortium for Citizens with Disabilities Employment and Training Task Force Statement of Principles on Employment of People with Disabilities*. Washington, D.C., November.

[7] Coutu, Marie-France, Raymond Baril, Marie José Durand, Daniel Côté&AnnickRouleau. ((2007). "Representations: An Important Key to Understanding Workers' Coping Behaviors during Rehabilitation and the Return-to-Work Process." *Journal of Occupational Rehabilitation,* vol. *17*, no.3. 522-544.

[8] Denny-Brown, Noelle, Boyd Gilman, Gilbert Gimm, Henry Ireys& Sarah Croake. (2009). "The Demonstration to Maintain Independence and Employment: Implications for National Health Care Reform." *Mathematica Policy Research Inc. Working with Disability Work and Insurance in Brief*, no. 10. Princeton, N.J., December.

[9] Goodman, Nanette J., David C. Stapleton, Gina A. Livermore & Bonnie O'Day. (2007). *The Health Care Financing Maze for Working-Age People with Disabilities.* January.

[10] Integrated Benefits Institute. (2008). *Employer Incentives for Workforce Health and Productivity.* San Francisco, Calif..

[11] The Lewin Group. (2009). *ASPE Technical Expert Panel on Earlier*

Intervention for Serious Mental Illness: Summary of Major Themes. Falls Church, Va., May.

[12] Livermore, Gina, Allison Roche & Sarah Prenovitz. (2009). *Work Activity and Use of Employment Supports Under the Original Ticket to Work Regulations: SSI and DI Beneficiaries with Work-Related Goals and Expectations.* Mathematica Policy Research, Inc. Prepared for the Social Security Administration, Office of Retirement and Disability Policy. October.

[13] MacDonald, Bryon R. & Megan O'Neil. (2006). *Being American: the Way Out of Poverty.* World Institute on Disability. Oakland, Calif., June.

[14] Mitra, Sophie. (2009). "Temporary and Partial Disability Programs in Nine Countries: What Can the United States Learn From Other Countries?" *Journal of Disability Policy Studies*, vol. *20*, no 1.(June): 14-27.

[15] National Council on Disability. (2007). Empowerment for Americans with Disabilities: Breaking Barriers to Careers and Full Employment. Washington, D.C., October.

[16] —*The Current State of Health Care for People with Disabilities.* (2009). Washington, D.C., September.

[17] —*The State of 21st Century Financial Incentives for Americans with Disabilities.* (2008). Washington, D.C., August.

[18] Palan, Martha A., Lynn Elinson& William D. Frey. (2007). *Evaluation of Disability Employment Policy Demonstration Programs: Task 10: A Synthesis of Key Findings, Issues, and Lessons Learned – Customized Employment Program Priority Area. Prepared for the U.S. Department of Labor, Office of Disability Employment Policy.* Westat: October.

[19] Social Security Administration. (2010). The 2010 Red Book: A Summary Guide to Employment Supports For Persons With Disabilities Under The Social Security Disability Insurance And Supplemental Security Income Programs. Baltimore, Md.

[20] —*Annual Report on Section 234 Demonstration Projects.* June 2009.

[21] Social Security Advisory Board. (2006). *A Disability System for the 21st Century.* Washington, D.C., September.

[22] Silverstein, Robert.(2000). "Emerging Disability Policy Framework: A Guidepost for Analyzing Public Policy," Center for the Study and Advancement of Disability Policy. *Iowa Law Review,* vol. 85, 1691-1797.

[23] Stapleton, David C., Bonnie L. O'Day, Gina A. Livermore & Andrew J. Imparato. (2006). "Dismantling the Poverty Trap: Disability Policy for

the Twenty-First Century." *The Milbank Quarterly*, vol. *84*, no.4, 701-732.

[24] Stapleton, David, Richard Burkhauser, Peiyun She, Robert R. Weathers II & Gina Livermore. (2009). "Income Security for Workers: A Stressed Support System in Need of Innovation." *Journal of Disability Policy Studies,* vol. *19*, no. 4, 204-220.

[25] Stapleton, David. (2007). "*Transforming Disability Policy*." Presented to the United States Senate Committee on Finance Hearing on Barriers to Work for Individuals Receiving Social Security Disability Benefits. Washington, D.C., June 21.

[26] Stapleton, David & Su Liu. (2009). "Will Health Care Reform Increase the Employment of People with Disabilities?" *Mathematica Policy Research, Inc. Disability Policy Research Brief*, no. 09-04. Princeton, N.J., November.

[27] Suter, Sue. (2009). *Testimony of Sue Suter, Associate Commissioner for Employment Support Programs Social Security Administration. Presented* before the U.S. House Committee on Ways and Means. Washington, D.C., May 19.

[28] Teleki, Stephanie, et al. (2006). *Research Colloquium on Workers' Compensation Medical Benefit Delivery and Return to Work.* RAND Corporation. Prepared for the California Commission on Health and Safety and Workers' Compensation. Santa Monica, Calif..

[29] Ticket to Work and Work Incentives Advisory Panel. (2007). *Building on the Ticket: A New Paradigm for Investing in Economic Self-Sufficiency for People with Significant Disabilities. Final Report to the President and Congress, Year Eight of the Panel.* Washington, D.C., December.

Improving Incentives for Employers, Insurers, and Service Providers

[1] Akabas, Sheila H., Donald E. Galvin & Lauren B. Gates. (1992). *Disability Management a Complete System to Reduce Costs, Increase Productivity, Meet Employee Needs, and Ensure Legal Compliance.* AMACOM, April.

[2] American College of Occupational & Environmental Medicine. (2007). *Ensuring Quality of Care in Worker's Compensation Programs: Fair*

Fee Schedules and Evidence-Based Guidelines. Elk Grove Village, Ill., July.

[3] Burkhauser, Richard V., Mary C. Daly & Philip R. de Jong. (2008). "Curing the Dutch Disease: Lessons for U.S. Disability Policy." *Michigan Retirement Research Center*, WP- 2008- 188. Ann Arbor, Mich., September.

[4] Burkhauser, Richard, Maximilian D. Schmeiser& Robert R. Weathers II. (2009). *The Importance of Anti-Discrimination and Workers' Compensation Laws on the Provision of Workplace Accommodations Following the Onset of a Disability*. October.

[5] Burton, John F. Jr. & Monroe Berkowitz. (1971). "Objectives Other Than Income Maintenance for Workmen's Compensation." *The Journal of Risk and Insurance*, vol. *38*, no. 3: 343-355.

[6] Carruthers, Marcia. (2008). "DMEC 2008 Employer Behavior Risk Survey." *Disability Management Employer Coalition*. June.

[7] CESSI. *Survey of Employer Perspectives on the Employment of People with Disabilities*. (2008). Prepared for the U.S. Department of Labor, Office of Disability Employment Policy. November.

[8] Dowd, Bryan et al. (2010). "The Economic Impact of a Disability Prevention Program." *Journal of Occupational and Environmental Medicine*, vol. *52*, no. 1 (January): 15-21.

[9] Franche, Renée-Louise et al. (2005). "Workplace-based return-to-work interventions: A systematic review of the quantitative literature." *Journal of Occupational Rehabilitation*, vol. *15*, no. 4 (December): 607-631.

[10] Schultz, Izabela Z. & Robert J. Gatchel, eds. (2005). *Handbook of Complex Occupational Disability Claims: Early Risk Identification, Intervention, and Prevention*. Springer:.

[11] Stapleton, David, Richard Burkhauser, Peiyun She, Robert R. Weathers II & Gina Livermore. (2009). "Income Security for Workers: A Stressed Support System in Need of Innovation." *Journal of Disability Policy Studies*, vol. *19* no. 4: 204-220.

[12] U.S. Department of Labor. (2010). Office of Disability Employment Policy. "Tax Incentives for Providing Business Accessibility." Washington, D.C. http://www.dol.gov/odep/pubs/fact/tifpba.htm (accessed on February 11).

Providing Education and Tools to Employers, Insurers, and Service Providers

[1] American College of Occupational and Environmental Medicine. (2008). *The Personal Physician's Role in Helping Patients with Medical Conditions Stay at Work or Return to Work.*

[2] American College of Occupational and Environmental Medicine Special Committee on Health, Productivity and Disability Management. (2009). "Healthy Workforce/Healthy Economy: The Role of Health, Productivity, and Disability Management in Addressing the Nation's Health Care Crisis." *Journal of Occupational and Environmental Medicine*, vol. *51*, no.1 114-119.

[3] American College of Occupational and Environmental Medicine and the Washington State Department of Labor and Industries. (2004). *Attending Doctor's Return to Work Desk Reference*. June.

[4] Assistive Technology Industry Association and the U.S. Business Leadership Network. (2007). *Roadmaps for Enhancing Employment of Persons with Disabilities through Accessible Technology*. Developed by participants at the Business Dialogue on Accessible Technology and Disability Employment. Orlando, Florida. September.

[5] Carruthers, Marcia. (2008). "DMEC 2008 Employer Behavioral Risk Survey." *Disability Management Employer Coalition*. June.

[6] CESSI. *Survey of Employer Perspectives on the Employment of People with Disabilities*. Prepared for the U.S. Department of Labor, Office of Disability Employment Policy. (2008). November.

[7] EarnWorks.com. EarnWorks.com: America's Choice for Qualified Workers. (2010). www.earnworks.com/businesscase/index.asp (accessed on April 21).

[8] Elinson, Lynn & William D. Frey. (2005). *Evaluation of Disability Employment Policy Demonstration Programs. Task 10: Interim Report on ODEP Demonstration Programs: Accomplishments and Issues Identified by the Independent Evaluation. Prepared for the Department of Labor Office of Disability Employment Policy*. Westat: June.

[9] Employer's Forum on Disability. *Realizing Potential: Disability Confidence*. (2010). http://www.realising-potential.org/ disability-confidence (accessed on June 8).

[10] Franche, Renée-Louise et al. (2005). "Workplace-based return-to-work interventions: A systematic review of the quantitative literature." *Journal of Occupational Rehabilitation,* vol. *15*, no. 4 (December): 607-

631.
[11] Habeck, Rochelle, Marcy Feuerstein & Larry Hickey. (2008). *Workforce Retention, Absence and Disability Management: Summary of DMEC/VCU Survey*. Virginia Commonwealth University Rehabilitation Research and Training Center on Workplace Supports and Job Retention. Presented to DMEC 13th Annual International Absence and Disability Management Conference. Denver, Colorado, August.
[12] Institute for Research on Labor and Employment, University of California at Berkeley. (2010). *Helping Injured Employees Return to Work: Practical Guidance under Workers' Compensation and Disability Rights Laws in California*. Prepared for California Commission on Health and Safety and Workers' Compensation. February.
[13] Integrated Benefits Institute. (2010). *Health + Productivity at Work*. www.ibiweb.org (accessed on June 19).
[14] Job Accommodation Network. (2009). U.S. Department of Labor, Office of Disability Employment Policy. *Workplace Accommodation: Low Cost, High Impact*. Morgantown, W.V., September.
[15] KosnyAgnieszka et al. (2006). "Early Healthcare Provider Communication with Patients and Their Workplace Following a Lost-Time Claim for an Occupational Musculoskeletal Injury." *Journal of Occupational Rehabilitation,* vol. *16*, No. 1 (March): 27-39.
[16] Krause Niklas, Lisa K. Dasinger& Frank Neuhauser. (1998). "Modified Work and Return to Work: A Review of the Literature." *Journal of Occupational Rehabilitation,* vol. *8*, No. 2: 113–139.
[17] National Council on Disability. (2007). *Empowerment for Americans with Disabilities: Breaking Barriers to Careers and Full Employment*. Washington, D.C., October.
[18] National Disability Rights Network. (2009). *Roadmaps II for Enhancing Employment of Persons with Disabilities through Accessible Technology*. Developed by Participants in the Assistive Technology Collaborative. January.
[19] Oregon Business Leadership Network. (2010). *Employment and Disability Business Case*. http://www.obln.org/BUScase.htm (accessed on April 5).
[20] Palan, Martha A, Lynn Elinson& William D. Frey. (2007). *Evaluation of Disability Employment Policy Demonstration Programs: Task 10: A Synthesis of Key Findings, Issues, and Lessons Learned – Customized Employment Program Priority Area*. Prepared for the U.S. Department of Labor, Office of Disability Employment Policy. Westat: October.

[21] Schultz, Izabela Z & Robert J. Gatchel, eds. (2005). *Handbook of Complex Occupational Disability Claims: Early Risk Identification, Intervention, and Prevention*, 1st ed. Springer:.

[22] U.S. Department of Defense. (2010). *Computer/Electronics Accommodations Program* (CAP). *http://www.tricare.mil/CAP/* About_us/(accessed on March 10).

Related GAO Products

Federal Disability Assistance: Wide Array of Programs Needs to Be Examined in Light of 21st Century Challenges. GAO-05-626. Washington, D.C.: June 2, 2005.

Federal Disability Programs: More Strategic Coordination Could Help Overcome Challenges to Needed Transformation. GAO-08-635. Washington, D.C.: May 20, 2008.

High Risk Series: An Update. GAO-09-271. Washington, D.C.: January 2009.

Highlights of a GAO Forum: Modernizing Federal Disability Policy. GAO-07-934SP. Washington, D.C.: August 3, 2007.

SSA Disability:Return-to-Work Strategies From Other Systems May Improve Federal Programs. GAO/HEHS-96-133. Washington, D.C.: July 11, 1996.

End Notes

[1]According to Bureau of Labor Statistics labor force data from the Current Population Survey.

[2]See GAO, *High-Risk Series: An Update*, GAO-09-271 (Washington, D.C.: January 2009).

[3]See GAO, *Federal Disability Assistance: Wide Array of Programs Needs to be Examined in Light of 21st Century Challenges*, GAO-05-626 (Washington, D.C.: June 2, 2005).

[4]See GAO, *Federal Disability Programs: More Strategic Coordination Could Help Overcome Challenges to Needed Transformation*, GAO-08-635 (Washington, D.C.: May 20, 2008).

[5]Although we obtained information from employers through our surveys, the employers we contacted were not able to attend our forum.

[6]In addition to employers, participants discussed possible actions for improving education, tools and incentives for insurers and providers of services, such as health care or employment services, but ultimately focused on proposed actions for employers.

[7]For the purposes of this report, we define "working age" as between 18 and 64 years old.

[8]Estimate based on Cornell University Disability Statistics analysis of 2008 U.S. Census American Community Survey (ACS) data for the noninstitutionalized population. This estimate has a range of plus or minus 0.31 percentage points. The ACS definition of

disability is based on six questions. A person is coded as having a disability if he, she or a proxy respondent answers affirmatively for one or more of these six disability categories: (1) hearing, (2) visual, (3) cognitive, (4) ambulatory, (5) self-care, or (6) independent living.

[9]Cornell University Disability Statistics analysis of 2008 ACS data for the noninstitutionalized population. This estimate has a range of plus or minus 0.18 percentage points.

[10]This analysis used 2004 National Beneficiary Survey data. For more information, see Gina Livermore, *Earnings and Work Expectations of Social Security Disability Beneficiaries*, Mathematica Policy Research, Inc., Disability Policy Research Brief Number 08-01 (2008).

[11]The World Health Organization's International Classification of Functioning, Disability, and Health (ICF), which was endorsed at the 54th World Health Assembly 2001, embodies this definition of disability. The ICF model explicitly recognizes that the health and level of function of an individual can be dynamic and affected by personal and environmental factors. For more information, also see Marilyn J. Field and Alan M. Jette, eds. *The Future of Disability in America*, Institute of Medicine of the National Academies (Washington, D.C.: National Academies Press, 2007).

[12]For example, see Job Accommodation Network, *Workplace Accommodation: Low Cost, High Impact,* prepared for the Department of Labor's Office of Disability Employment Policy, 2009. Also see Martha A. Palan, Lynn Elinson, and William D. Frey, *Evaluation of Disability Employment Policy Demonstration Programs: Task 10: A Synthesis of Key Findings, Issues, and Lessons Learned–Customized Employment Program Priority Area*, prepared for the Department of Labor, Office of Disability Employment Policy (Westat: 2007).

[13]American College of Occupational and Environmental Medicine, *ACOEM Guideline: Preventing Needless Work Disability by Helping People Stay Employed* (2006).

[14]For more information, see GAO, *SSA Disability: Return-to-Work Strategies From Other Systems May Improve Federal Programs,* GAO/HEHS 96-133 (Washington D.C.: July 11, 1996). Also see Sheila H. Akabas, Lauren B. Gates, Donald E. Galvin, et al., *Disability Management: A Complete System to Reduce Costs, Increase Productivity, Meet Employee Needs, and Ensure Legal Compliance* (American Management Association: 1992).

[15]Employers can provide disability insurance to their employees by purchasing or subsidizing employees' purchase of insurance from insurance companies or through self-insuring under the Employee Retirement Income Security Act of 1974 (ERISA) (29 U.S.C. § 1001et seq.). Disability insurance benefit plans generally fall into two categories: short-term or long-term (which generally continues until retirement or a specified age).

[16]This estimate is from the Bureau of Labor Statistics' 2009 National Compensation Survey. The survey includes civilian workers in the private nonfarm economy, except those in private households, and workers in the public sector, except the federal government. Five states—California, Hawaii, New Jersey, New York, and Rhode Island—and Puerto Rico have mandated short-term disability coverage for qualifying individuals. California and Rhode Island do not require employer contributions; Hawaii, New Jersey, and New York do. Congressional Research Service, *Leave Benefits in the United States,* RL34088 (2009).

[17]Americas Health Insurance Plans, *Disability Income Insurance: Group and Worksite Issues* (2003). In most instances, workers' compensation covers injuries that are caused, in whole or in part, by work.

[18]Individuals who qualify for cash assistance based on disability receive benefits through SSDI if they previously worked in employment covered by Social Security for a sufficient period of time, through SSI if they are below a designated income level, or through both if they meet the eligibility criteria for both programs.

[19]SSA considers individuals to have a disability if SSA determines they cannot perform their previous work and cannot adjust to other work due to a medically determinable physical or mental impairment and other relevant factors, and the disability is expected to last for at least 1 year or result in death. The term "substantial gainful activity" is used to describe a significant level of physical and/or mental work activity and income or earnings threshold

that is established by regulation and recalculated regularly using an established formula. In 2010, the substantial gainful activity income threshold was $1,000 per month for adults who were disabled but not blind. Those earning above this income threshold may become ineligible for continued SSDI benefits.

[20]It is too soon to determine how the Patient Protection and Affordable Care Act as amended by the Health Care and Education Reconciliation Act of 2010 (i.e., Health Care Reform) will impact access to health care for individuals with disabilities.

[21]Pub. L. No. 106-170 (1999). In addition to establishing the Ticket to Work program, the law also authorized demonstration projects designed to improve incentives for SSA beneficiaries to return to work. For more information about these demonstrations, see Social Security Administration, *Annual Report on Section 234 Demonstration Projects* (June 2009).

[22]Eligible beneficiaries are provided tickets to be used as vouchers to request vocational rehabilitation, employment, or other support services from the traditional state VR agencies or from new SSA-approved public or private service providers, which are referred to as employment networks (EN).

[23]For more information, see Gina Livermore, Allison Roche, and Sarah Prenovitz, *Work Activity and Use of Employment Supports Under the Original Ticket to Work Regulations: SSI and DI Beneficiaries with Work-Related Goals and Expectations,* Mathematica Policy Research, Inc., prepared for the Social Security Administration Office of Disability and Income Support Programs, October 2009.

[24]73 Fed. Reg. 29324 (May 20, 2008).

[25]Individuals are eligible for VR services if they have a physical or mental impairment that constitutes a substantial impediment to employment and can benefit from VR services; however, many state agencies operate under an "order of selection," meaning they lack sufficient resources to provide comprehensive services to all eligible individuals. When this is the case, federal regulations require the state to give priority to those who have the "most significant" disabilities, as determined by the state.

[26]GAO-05-626.

[27]Under Medicaid Buy-in, states have the option to extend Medicaid benefits to individuals with disabilities who work.

[28]Bureau of Labor Statistics, 2009 National Compensation Survey.

[29]Benefits counseling is currently provided by SSA through the Work Incentives Planning and Assistance (WIPA) programs. WIPA projects are funded by SSA and work with a variety of organizations to provide disability beneficiaries with information on employment and community resources that can support their return to work. WIPA is still evolving and Mathematica, which is evaluating the program under contract with SSA, has issued a report. See Mathematica Policy Research, Inc., *Work Activity and Use of Employment Supports Under the Original Ticket to Work Regulations: Process Evaluation of the Work Incentives Planning and Assistance Program* (Washington, D.C., February 2009).

[30]Additionally, usage of some existing tax incentives—such as the Disabled Access Credit and the Work Opportunity Tax Credit—is low and could be improved. For more information see, Bryon MacDonald and Megan O'Neil, *Being American: the Way Out of Poverty* (Oakland, Calif.: World Institute on Disability, 2006).

[31]Pub. L. No. 103-3 (1993).

[32]For examples of existing research in this area, see the following: EarnWorks.com, *Talent to Drive your Business' Success,* www.earnworks.com/businesscase/index.asp (accessed on April 21, 2010); the Integrated Benefits Institute, *Bringing Workforce Health and Productivity to the C-Suite,* http://ibiweb.org/ (accessed on April 22,2010); and the Oregon Business Leadership Network, *Business Case,* http://www.obln.org/BUScase.htm (accessed on April 5, 2010).

[33]Participants cited the example of a recent collaboration between Microsoft and Forrester Research to illustrate the power of using well-known and respected brands to get attention

from the business community. See Forrester Research Inc., *The Wide Range of Abilities and Its Impact on Computer Technology,* commissioned by Microsoft, Inc., 2004 and Forrester Research Inc., *Accessible Technology in Computing Examining Awareness, Use, and Future Potential,* commissioned by Microsoft, Inc., 2004.

[34]Participants cited the concept of "disability confidence" when discussing improvements in employer culture and employee comfort in disclosing disabilities. For more information, see the Employer's Forum on Disability, *Disability Confidence,* http://www.realising-potential.org/disability-confidence/ (accessed on June 8, 2010).

[35]Employers often cover or contribute to short-term costs such as paid sick leave, workers' compensation payments, short-term disability insurance and accommodations for their employees. Although some employers provide private long-term disability insurance to their employees, most only contribute to long-term costs of disability by indirectly funding the SSDI program through payroll taxes.

[36]For more information about experience rating in workers' compensation programs, see Richard Burkhauser, Maximilian D. Schmeiser and Robert R. Weathers II, *The Importance of Anti-Discrimination and Workers' Compensation Laws on the Provision of Workplace Accommodations Following the Onset of a Disability*, funded by the Department of Education, National Institute on Disability and Rehabilitation Research, October 2009. Also see John F. Burton Jr. and Monroe Berkowitz, "Objectives Other Than Income Maintenance for Workmen's Compensation," *The Journal of Risk and Insurance,* vol. 38, no. 3 (1971).

[37]These participants likened this approach to the system used in the Netherlands. For more information see Burkhauser, Richard V., Mary C. Daly, and Philip R. de Jong, "Curing the Dutch Disease: Lessons for U.S. Disability Policy," *Michigan Retirement Research Center,* WP- 2008- 188 (September 2008).

[38]Participants stated that the specific time period for these benefits would be determined through actuarial calculations but estimated that it would be approximately 1 to 3 years.

[39]Participants noted that in these cases, it would be appropriate and cost-effective for employers to facilitate the individuals' application for SSDI benefits.

[40]For more information on existing tax incentives, see GAO, *Business Tax Incentives: Incentives to Employ Workers with Disabilities Receive Limited Use and Have an Uncertain Impact,* GAO-03-39 (Washington, D.C.: Dec. 11, 2002); and the Office of Disability Employment Policy, *Tax Incentives for Providing Business Accessibility,* http://www.dol.gov/odep/pubs/fact/tifpba.htm (accessed on Feb. 11, 2010).

[41]See David Stapleton, Richard Burkhauser, Peiyun She, Robert R. Weathers II, and Gina Livermore, "Income Security for Workers: A Stressed Support System in Need of Innovation," *Journal of Disability Policy Studies*, vol. 19, no. 4 (2009): 204-220.

[42]For more information about the last three options, see National Council on Disability, *The Current State of Health Care for People with Disabilities* (September 2009); and American College of Occupational and Environmental Medicine, *ACOEM Guideline: Preventing Needless Work Disability by Helping People Stay Employed* (2006).

[43]GAO, *Federal Disability Programs: More Strategic Coordination Could Help Overcome Challenges to Needed Transformation*, GAO-08-635 (Washington, D.C.: May 20, 2008).

[44]Exec. Order No. 13,518, 74 Fed. Reg. 58,533 (Nov. 9, 2009).

[45]The federal government has the authority to use an alternate hiring process in order to expedite the hiring of certain individuals with disabilities. For example, government agencies can hire an individual for a position without first publicizing the job opening.

[46]Based on late changes to the forum's composition, we increased the forum size to 17 to help ensure sufficient balance in perspectives.

In: Work and Play for the Disabled: Research on... ISBN: 978-1-61122-463-4
Editor: Lauren S. Randow

Chapter 2

STUDENTS WITH DISABILITIES: MORE INFORMATION AND GUIDANCE COULD IMPROVE OPPORTUNITIES IN PHYSICAL EDUCATION AND ATHLETICS

United States Government Accountability Office

WHY GAO DID THIS STUDY

Research has established that physical activity and participation in athletics provides important health and social benefits for children. Certain federal laws help ensure that kindergarten-12th grade schools provide students with disabilities opportunities to participate in physical education (PE) and extracurricular athletics equal to those of their peers. However, national associations have questioned whether students with disabilities receive opportunities similar to their peers.

Regarding students with disabilities, GAO was asked to examine (1) what is known about the PE opportunities that schools provide, and how do schools provide these; (2) what is known about the extracurricular athletic opportunities that schools provide, and how do schools provide these; and (3) how the Department of Education (Education) assists states and schools in these areas. GAO analyzed federal survey data; reviewed relevant federal laws and regulations; and interviewed state, district, and school officials in selected states, as well as parents and disability association officials.

What GAO Recommends

To improve the opportunities for students with disabilities in PE and athletics, GAO recommends that the Secretary of Education facilitate information sharing among states and schools on ways to provide opportunities and clarify schools' responsibilities under federal law. Education agreed with both of our recommendations.

What GAO Found

Schools provide students with and without disabilities similar opportunities to participate in PE but face challenges when serving students with disabilities. Students with disabilities spend similar amounts of time in PE class and exercising in class as students without disabilities, according to national data and GAO site visits. Most students with disabilities take PE with other students in general PE classes. To facilitate their participation, teachers may make accommodations for some students, such as providing additional modeling or repetition. Many state, district, and school officials GAO interviewed cited teacher preparation and budget constraints as key challenges to serving students with disabilities in general PE classes. For example, they said general PE teachers need more training opportunities on working specifically with students with disabilities, yet resources for training are not always available.

Source: MnPrepPhoto.com © (2008).

Adapted Athletics

Limited national data suggest that students with disabilities participate in extracurricular athletics, but do not distinguish whether these opportunities are offered through schools or community programs. Among the schools GAO visited, students with disabilities participated in athletics at varying rates, but at consistently lower rates than students without disabilities. Several factors, such as a student's disability type or outreach to students, may affect participation. Some schools or districts GAO interviewed provided opportunities by partnering with community programs or offering athletics designed specifically for students with disabilities, such as wheelchair basketball. District and school officials GAO interviewed cited a lack of information on ways to expand athletic opportunities, lack of clarity regarding schools' responsibilities, and budget constraints as key challenges.

Education has provided little information or guidance on PE or extracurricular athletics for students with disabilities, and some states and districts GAO interviewed said more would be useful. According to agency officials, Education has not provided much information or guidance because it has targeted its limited resources on other areas, such as monitoring priorities specified in federal law. Officials from several states and many districts said they could benefit from Education helping states and schools to share information on practices or resources regarding PE and athletics for students with disabilities. Officials from districts and disability groups also said more clarification from Education on schools' responsibilities under federal law on extracurricular athletics for students with disabilities would be useful.

ABBREVIATIONS

ADA	Americans with Disabilities Act of 1990, as amended
Education	Department of Education
IDEA	Individuals with Disabilities Education Act
IEP	Individualized Education Program
NFHS	National Federation of State High School Associations
NLTS2	National Longitudinal Transition Study-2
OCR	Office for Civil Rights
OSDFS	Office of Safe and Drug-Free Schools
OSEP	Office of Special Education Programs
PE	physical education
SEELS	Special Education Elementary Longitudinal Study

SHPPS	School Health Policies and Programs Study
YRBS	Youth Risk Behavior Survey

June 23, 2010

The Honorable Tom Harkin
United States Senate

The Honorable George Miller
Chairman
Committee on Education and Labor
House of Representatives

The Honorable Carolyn McCarthy
Chairwoman
Subcommittee on Healthy Families and Communities
Committee on Education and Labor
House of Representatives

The Honorable Chris Van Hollen
House of Representatives

The health and social benefits of physical activity and athletic participation for children are well established. These benefits may be even more important for children with disabilities, including those with cognitive and physical disabilities who have a greater risk of being sedentary and having associated health conditions, such as obesity and reduced cardiovascular fitness.[1] Studies have shown that for students with disabilities, regular physical activity may help control or slow the progression of chronic disease, improve muscular strength, control body weight, and enhance students' psychological well-being through additional social ties and improved self-confidence and self-esteem.[2]

Certain federal laws and regulations help ensure that children with disabilities are provided opportunities to participate in physical education (PE) and extracurricular athletics that are equal to those of other children.[3] The Individuals with Disabilities Education Act (IDEA)[4] mandates that states receiving federal grants under the act generally ensure that eligible elementary and secondary school students with disabilities receive a free appropriate public education which is defined as certain special education and related services. Students with a range of disabilities are protected under IDEA, including those with cognitive or emotional disabilities and those with visual, hearing, or orthopedic impairments. Another key federal law protecting students with disabilities is Section 504 of the Rehabilitation Act of 1973 (Section 504),[5] which prohibits entities that receive federal funds, such as elementary and secondary schools, from discriminating against otherwise qualified individuals with disabilities.[6] Under the implementing regulations for both IDEA and Section 504, schools are required to provide students with disabilities equal opportunity for participation in extracurricular activities, which often include athletics.[7] In its administration of these federal laws, the Department of Education (Education) provides oversight and assistance to states and local education agencies, including administering federal funds, monitoring IDEA and Section 504 compliance, and providing guidance and technical assistance.

Despite the health and social benefits of physical activity and the existence of these federal laws, national associations have raised questions about whether elementary and secondary schools are providing students with disabilities similar opportunities in PE and extracurricular athletics as compared to the opportunities of their peers without disabilities. In light of these concerns, you asked us to address the following:

1. what is known about the PE opportunities that schools provide to students with disabilities, and how do schools provide these opportunities;
2. what is known about the extracurricular athletic opportunities that schools provide to students with disabilities, and how do schools provide these opportunities; and
3. how Education assists states and schools to provide opportunities in PE and extracurricular athletics to students with disabilities.

To address these issues, we examined pertinent data from four nationally representative studies that provided the most current national survey data available for our purposes: the 2006 School Health Policies and Programs Study (SHPPS), the 2005 Youth Risk Behavior Survey (YRBS), 2001 data from the National Longitudinal Transition Study-2 (NLTS2), and 2000 data from the Special Education Elementary Longitudinal Study (SEELS).[8] We reviewed the methods and survey design used in these studies and, through interviews with knowledgeable agency officials and our own analyses, determined that the data we used were sufficiently reliable for our purposes. While more recent data are available from NLTS2 and SEELS, we determined that the data collected during the first wave of these two longitudinal studies were more reliable for the purposes of generating estimates of student participation in PE and extracurricular athletics. In addition, we conducted site visits in five states (California, Florida, Maryland, Minnesota, and New Jersey) and interviewed officials from state departments of education and state athletic associations, school districts, and schools. We also interviewed teachers, coaches, parents, and students. In each state, we visited two school districts and four schools. In addition, we conducted phone interviews with officials from state agencies and district offices selected in Georgia and Texas. We chose these seven states because they had relatively higher numbers of students with disabilities nationwide and varied in whether they had policies requiring elementary, middle, and secondary schools to teach PE, and geographic location.[9] We chose school districts that varied in their percentages of students with disabilities, socio-economic status, and classification as urban, rural, or suburban. In deciding between multiple states or districts that met our selection criteria, we purposely chose some that external stakeholders recommended as having innovative or promising practices. To obtain information from parents, we set up informal meetings with assistance from staff in Parent Training and Information Centers in each state we visited. The information and data we gathered from these site visits are not generalizable to all states and districts. In addition to our site visits, we interviewed representatives from 21 national associations, community organizations, and experts in the areas of disability, health, PE, special education, and athletics. We also interviewed Education officials about Education's relevant oversight and assistance efforts and reviewed relevant federal laws, regulations, guidance, and other agency documentation and data. See appendix I for additional information on our methodology.

We conducted this performance audit from June 2009 through June 2010 in accordance with generally accepted government auditing standards. Those standards require that we plan and perform the audit to obtain sufficient, appropriate evidence to provide a reasonable basis for our findings and conclusions based on our audit objectives. We believe that the evidence obtained provides a reasonable basis for our findings and conclusions based on our audit objectives.

BACKGROUND

IDEA and Section 504

IDEA authorizes federal funding for the needs of school-age children with a range of disabilities, such as specific learning disabilities, speech and language impairments, or mental retardation, who need special education services (see figure 1). In 2007-2008, students covered under IDEA made up about 13 percent of the nation's public prekindergarten through 12th grade school enrollment and, in fiscal year 2007, states received $10.8 billion in federal funds to provide services to school-age students.[10] To receive federal funds, states and local educational agencies must identify and evaluate children who have a disability and provide special education and related services, as well as supplementary aids and services when necessary, to those who are eligible. Such services and supports are formulated in an individualized education program (IEP), which is developed, discussed, and documented by a student's IEP team. An IEP team must generally include, among others, the parents of the child, a general education teacher, a special education teacher, and the child when appropriate. IDEA also requires the placement of students in the least restrictive environment—in which students with disabilities are educated with students without disabilities—to the maximum extent appropriate. Regarding PE, IDEA regulations specify that schools must generally provide opportunities for students to participate in regular or general PE classes or, in some cases, specially designed PE if determined by the IEP team. Regarding extracurricular athletics, districts and schools must take steps to provide services to give students with disabilities an opportunity to participate in extracurricular activities, which may include athletics, equal to that of other students.

Section 504 prohibits entities that receive federal financial assistance, including elementary and secondary (K-12) schools, from discriminating against otherwise qualified individuals with disabilities. The Americans with Disabilities Act of 1990, as amended (ADA) is also a broad antidiscriminatory law protecting individuals with disabilities. Education interprets the ADA and Section 504 in a similar manner. While IDEA students are covered under Section 504, other students who are not covered under IDEA may still have a disability as defined under Section 504. Several of the most common disabilities of students included under Section 504, but not always covered under IDEA, are attention deficit hyperactivity disorder, diabetes, and asthma.[11] In 2006, about 444,000 students with disabilities were covered under 504, and not IDEA, based on the most recent estimates from Education. These students may have an education plan developed under Section 504 that sets forth their needed regular or special education and related aids and services, but the federal requirements for such a plan are much less detailed than for an IEP. Similar to IDEA, Education's Section 504 regulations require that students with disabilities be provided a free appropriate public education and learn alongside students without disabilities to the maximum extent appropriate. These Section 504 regulations also require that students with disabilities must be provided equal opportunities to participate in PE courses and extracurricular athletics. Unlike IDEA, however, Section 504 does not authorize any federal funding to schools to provide services to students. (See table 1 for more information on IDEA and Section 504.)

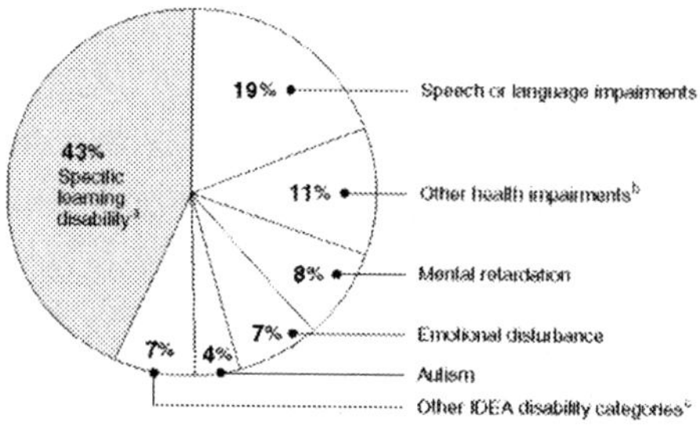

Source: GAO analysis of Fall 2007 Education data from states found on www.ideadata.org.

Note: Vermont data was not available this year and is not included in calculations for the chart. Numbers do not add to 100 percent due to rounding.

[a]According to IDEA regulations, a "specific learning disability" is a disorder in one or more of the basic psychological processes involved in understanding or in using language, spoken or written, that may affect the ability to listen, think, speak, read, write, spell, or to do mathematical calculations (e.g., dyslexia).

[b] According to IDEA regulations, "other health impairment" is considered as having limited strength, vitality, or alertness due to chronic or acute health problems (e.g., a heart condition or diabetes) that result in limited alertness to the educational environment and adversely affect a child's educational performance.

[c] Other IDEA disability categories include multiple disabilities (2 percent), developmental delays (2 percent), hearing impairments (1 percent), orthopedic impairments (1 percent), visual impairments (0.4 percent), traumatic brain injury (0.4 percent), and deaf-blindness (less than 0.1 percent).

Figure 1. IDEA Students Ages 6-21 by Disability Category in 2007: 50 States and District of Columbia

Table 1. Relevant Federal Laws and Requirements Regarding Students with Disabilities

	Individuals with Disabilities Education Act (IDEA)	Section 504 of the Rehabilitation Act of 1973
General purpose	Provides federal funds to state and local educational agencies to guarantee special education and related servi-ces to eligible children with disabilities.	Prohibits discrimination on the basis of disability in programs or activities that receive federal financial assistance.
General coverage	Children, generally ages 3 through 21, with a disability who need special education and related services.	Individuals of all ages who have a disability as defined in the act.
Disability definition	A child with a disability in one of many specific categ-ories, such as speech or lang-uage impairment, emotional disturbance, or mental retar-dation, who needs special education and related services.	A person who has a physical or mental impairment that substantially limits one or more major life activeties.[a] Major life activities include walking, communicating, working, reading, learning, concentrating, and thinking.
Approximate numbers of K-12 students	About 5.9 million children ages 6-21 in Fall 2007 for the 50 states and the District of Columbia.	IDEA students are gener-ally protected under Section 504. In addition, according to its most recent available data, Education estimated that about 444,000 K-12 students were covered under Section 504, but not IDEA, in 2006.
Provides fede-ral funding	Yes	No
Physical education requirements	Public education agencies must make PE available to children with disabilities unless the school does not offer it to nondisabled students in the same grades. Public education agencies must also provide a child with a disability the opportunity to participate in the regular PE program that is available to	Entities that provide extracurricular services and activities, which may include physical recreational athletics, must afford students with disabilities an opportunity for participation in such services and activities equal to that of other students. In providing PE courses and athletics to any of its students,

Table 1. (Continued)

	Individuals with Disabilities Education Act (IDEA)	Section 504 of the Rehabilitation Act of 1973
	Nondisabled children unless (1) the child is enrolled full-time in a separate facility or (2) the child needs specially designed PE as prescribed in the child's IEP.	entities may not discriminate on the basis of a student's disability and must provide quailfied students an equal opportunity to participate. Separate or different PE and athletic activities may be offered. However, quailfied students must continue to have the opportunity to compete for teams or to participate in courses that are not separate or different.
Extracurricular athletics requirements	Each public agency must take steps, including the provision of supplementary aids and services determined appropriate and necessary, to provide nonacademic and extracurricular services and activities, which may include athletics. These must be provided in the manner necess-ary to afford children with disabilities an opportunity for participation in those services and activities equal to that of other students	
Administering office	Office of Special Education Programs makes formula grants to states and overseesimplementation of IDEA, and it makes discretionary grants in special education program areas.	Office for Civil Rights with 12 regional enforcement offices.

Source: GAO analysis of relevant federal laws and regulations, and other agency documents.

[a]The definition of an individual with a disability also includes someone who has a record of such impairment or is regarded as having such an impairment.

Federal and State Responsibilities

At the federal level, Education is responsible for administering IDEA, as well as Section 504, as it applies to many educational institutions. The Office of Special Education Programs (OSEP) allocates federal funds to states for their implementation of IDEA programs and monitors states' ability to provide a free, appropriate public education. For example, states must report to OSEP the amount of time that students who are covered under IDEA spend in their state's general education classes, including PE. The Office for Civil Rights (OCR), through its headquarters and 12 regional offices, carries out enforcement activities related to Section 504, the ADA, and other antidiscrimination laws.[12] These activities include investigating complaints of discrimination on the basis of race, color, national origin, sex, disability, or age. OSEP and OCR also help states and schools meet their federal requirements and improve the quality of education by issuing policy guidance, disseminating information, and providing technical assistance to individual institutions. Education funds and oversees numerous national and regional research and technical assistance providers, such as regional educational laboratories and national clearinghouses that disseminate information, research, and other support to policymakers and educators at the state and local levels. For example, the Office of Special Education and Rehabilitative Services, which includes OSEP, supports a network of more than 40 national technical assistance centers, each with a focus on some aspect of special education.

At state and district levels, various parties may be involved in providing students with opportunities in PE and extracurricular athletics. For instance, many states have requirements regarding their districts' provision of PE, according to data from the Centers for Disease Control and Prevention and the National Association of State Boards of Education. However, policies may vary by state or district, such as the required grades in which PE should be offered, the number of minutes students should be in class, or the specific content and curriculum areas that should be taught. For extracurricular athletics, the National Federation of State High School Associations (NFHS) is the national body that writes the rules of competition for most high school interscholastic sports—the main form of extracurricular athletic competition in schools, which includes varsity and junior-varsity level teams. In turn, each state has its own state high school athletic association which is a voluntary member of the NFHS. According to an NFHS official, NFHS does not establish standards or policies specifically regarding students with disabilities and each state athletic association develops its own standards and policies. In addition, most state high school athletic associations are not part of state departments of education, but are private organizations, according to NFHS officials.

SCHOOLS PROVIDE STUDENTS WITH AND WITHOUT DISABILITIES SIMILAR OPPORTUNITIES IN PE, BUT FACE CHALLENGES SERVINGSTUDENTS IN GENERAL PE CLASSES

Schools Provide Similar Opportunities in PE to Students with and without Disabilities

Students with disabilities generally attend PE class about the same amount of time as students without disabilities, according to national data and our site visits. Estimates from YRBS 2005 on high school students indicate that students with physical disabilities or long-term health problems attend PE classes for approximately the same amount of time as those without disabilities. For example, 29 percent of students with physical disabilities or long-term health problems attend PE class 5 days a week compared to 34 percent of students without disabilities (see figure 2).[13] In 12 schools and seven districts we visited, officials also told us that most students with disabilities are in PE class the same amount of time as students without disabilities. Officials from a few schools said that they actually provide a greater amount of instruction time in PE for some students with disabilities who have specific needs and take both general PE classes and specialized PE classes. National data show that among districts that require PE, many have policies allowing student to be exempt from PE due to long-term physical, medical, or cognitive disabilities. However, exemptions for students with disabilities were very rare according to officials in the 20 schools we visited.[14] Rather than exempting students with disabilities from PE class entirely, a few schools we visited excuse some students from certain activities. For example, officials from one high school in New Jersey we visited told us that a few students with medical conditions, such as asthma, may be exempt from particular activities but that they are given alternative activities.

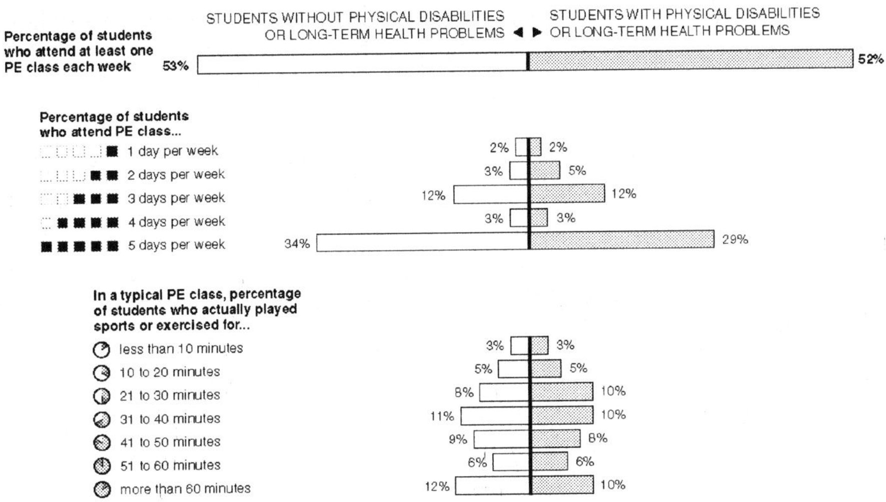

Source: GAO analysis of YRBS, 2005.

Note: Differences in estimates of the number of days attending PE and in time spent exercising are not statistically significant at the 95 percent confidence level among students with and without physical disabilities or long-term health problems. YRBS estimates have 95 percent confidence intervals within plus or minus 7 percentage points unless otherwise noted.

Figure 2. Number of Days per Week Students with and without Disabilities Attend PE Class and Minutes Spent Exercising or Playing Sports in an Average PE Class

Schools generally provided students with and without disabilities comparable opportunities to participate in PE, according to national data and our site visits. According to 2005 YRBS estimates, students with and without physical disabilities or long-term health problems spend similar amounts of time actually engaged in physical activity per class. For instance, 8 percent of students with physical disabilities or long-term health problems spend 41 to 50 minutes in a typical PE class exercising or playing sports compared to 9 percent of students without these disabilities.[15] Many district and schools officials, as well as some students we spoke with, said that students with disabilities often participate in PE to the same extent as their peers without disabilities. In addition, almost all state, district, and school officials we spoke with reported they rarely received complaints about PE from parents of students with disabilities. Several state and district officials said that while they hear complaints from parents in other areas, PE is generally an area in which parents seem satisfied.

Various factors may affect students' experience in PE, such as their school level (e.g., elementary or middle) or their type of disability. For instance, some parents and school officials said that PE teachers in elementary school may be able to more easily integrate students with disabilities in their classes than those in secondary schools because peers in elementary school are more accepting, the equipment is more varied, and there is less focus on competitive games than in secondary school, which may be harder for students with disabilities to participate. Some district and school officials also said that middle school can be particularly difficult for some students with disabilities who may have more difficulty changing into PE uniforms or opening combination locks on their PE lockers. However, some schools overcame these challenges by waiving their PE uniform policy or providing key locks to accommodate students with disabilities. In addition, some parents and school officials noted that whether a student has a physical or cognitive disability may affect their experience. For example, officials in one school said that while students with physical impairments required more accommodations, they also may have an easier time expressing their needs than students with cognitive disabilities. On the other hand, many district and school officials told us that students with emotional or behavioral disabilities usually participated in the same activities as other students and often excelled physically. Some noted that PE class can provide them a physical outlet that helps them focus their energy.

Schools Use Various Approaches to Provide PE to Students with Disabilities, but Most Included Students in the General PE Class

National data indicate that most students with disabilities who took PE did so in general education classes with students who do not have disabilities. Specifically, 92 percent of students with disabilities in grades 1 through 7 took PE in general education classes, according to SEELS estimates. In grades 7 through 12, 88 percent of students with disabilities took PE in general education classes, according to NLTS2 estimates.[16] Similarly, in most of the schools we visited, the majority of IDEA students received PE in a general classroom without any accommodations or modifications. Officials from a number of schools we visited told us that for some students with disabilities who are in special education classes, PE is the one general education class that they attend on a regular basis. School and district officials also noted that the emphasis on educating students with disabilities in an inclusive environment with their peers without disabilities in all subjects also contributes to the high numbers of students in general PE classes.

STATE GUIDANCE ON PE CLASSROOM ADAPTATIONS

Source: New Jersey State Department of Education.

A section of New Jersey's Comprehensive Health Education and Physical Education Curriculum Framework outlines instructional adaptations teachers and others may need to consider for students with disabilities in PE and health. The guidance outlines different types of adaptations and provides examples of these, such as

- instructional presentation (e.g., using visuals);
- classroom organization (e.g., regulating noise or lighting);
- student response (e.g., giving credit for improvement); and
- safety (e.g. establishing activity boundaries).

To facilitate participation for students with disabilities in general PE classes, teachers may make accommodations or modifications for students, which are often informal. According to 2006 SHPPS data and many teachers we interviewed, common informal adjustments that teachers use for students with disabilities in PE class include simplifying the instructional content, providing additional skill modeling or repetition, and having peers without disabilities assist in teaching or coaching (see figure 3). School officials said that these types of informal accommodations or modifications are generally not determined through the IEP process. In contrast, schools we visited said that more formal accommodations or modifications are usually determined through the IEP process and noted on a student's IEP. These may include modifying assessments (e.g., allowing students to have more time to take tests); using specialized equipment; or having individual aides or assistants work with students during class. For example, officials from a middle school in California told us that some students with disabilities receive accommodations when taking tests for all their classes, including PE, and this is written on students' IEPs. Similarly, officials from schools we visited who had individual aides help some students with disabilities in PE class said the use of these aides was also determined on a case-by-case basis through the IEP process.

MINNESOTA ADAPTED PE TEACHER CERTIFICATION

Source: Center on Disability Health and Adapted Physical Activity, University of Wisconsin-La Crosse.

- Under Minnesota state policies, adapted PE must be taught by a PE teacher with an additional adapted PE license based on our review of state documents and interviews with state officials.
- According to state officials, teacher training programs encourage prospective PE teachers to obtain this license to be more marketable, and thus, there are many more certified adapted PE teachers in the state than actual positions.

Some schools accommodate students with more severe motor development delays by providing specialized or "adapted" PE instruction, using various approaches. Nationally, less than 11 percent of students with disabilities under IDEA received adapted PE in 2000 and 2001, according to SEELS and NLTS2 estimates.[17] Among the schools and districts we visited, the provision of adapted PE varied. Officials from 8 of the 20 schools we visited reported that no students received adapted PE services at the time we visited. The remaining schools reported that between 2 and 29 percent of IDEA students—who represent most students with disabilities—received adapted PE. Many districts we visited told us that the provision of adapted PE for individual students was always determined through the IEP process. Districts in Minnesota also relied on standard statewide criteria to provide adapted PE, such as formal tests evaluating motor skills or fitness levels.

STRATEGIES USED BY MIAMI-DADE COUNTY PUBLIC SCHOOLS

Source: National Institutes of Health, Department of Health and Human Services.

- The district promotes the "I Can Do It, You Can Do It" program, sponsored by the National Institutes of Health in the Department of Health and Human Services. Students with physical or cognitive disabilities earn a Presidential Active Lifestyle Award if they participate in 30 minutes of activity 5 days a week for 6 weeks.
- The district also has a hybrid PE and sports program for students with disabilities. During the school day, students participate in activities such as wheelchair basketball or adapted sailing. The district has obtained specialized equipment and facility space through community partnerships, such as with the local sailing club and county golf course.

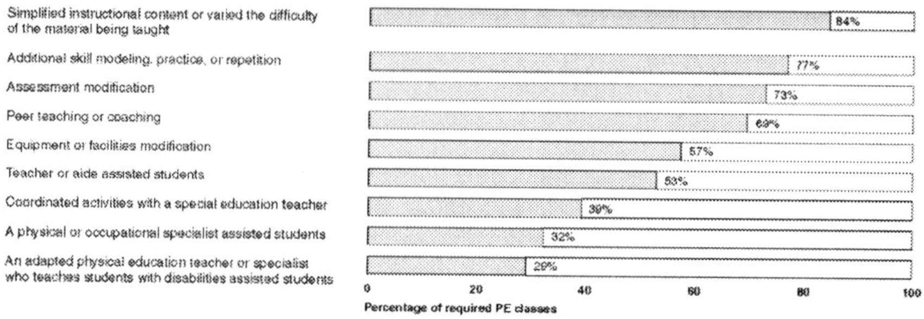

Source: SHPPS , 2006.

Note: According to SHPPS, these percentages pertain to teachers who taught required PE classes or courses in the 23 percent of these classes that had students with long-term physical, medical, or cognitive disabilities. Estimates have 95 percent confidence intervals within plus or minus 5.5 percentage points unless otherwise noted.

Figure 3. Strategies Used by PE Teachers to Accommodate Students with Disabilities in Required PE Classes

Schools we visited provide adapted PE using different approaches. Students may receive direct instruction from an adapted PE teacher, the adapted PE teacher may consult with the general PE teacher who actually provides the specific modifications or accommodations to the student, or schools may use a combination of both approaches. Some states require that adapted PE be taught by a PE teacher with a supplemental license, including California and Minnesota, based on state documents we reviewed and state officials we interviewed. Nationwide, 12 states offer or require a supplemental adapted PE license to teach adapted PE, according to the Center on Disability Health and Adapted Physical Activity.[18] Some adapted PE teachers travel to several schools to provide services in the districts we visited. In one district we visited in Florida, the sole adapted PE teacher overcame challenges in scheduling her time by having students who took adapted PE bussed to a central school so she could provide them with services. Some parents we spoke with were pleased with their children's adapted PE experiences, while others said that their experiences varied and depended on factors such as individual teaching styles and the extent to which students who received adapted PE were integrated into the general PE class.

Fewer students receive PE only in separate or self-contained classes as opposed to receiving PE in general classes with other students, according to national data and our site visits. Our estimates from SEELS indicate that 7 percent were in a self-contained special education classroom for PE in 2000.[19] Among eight districts we visited that could provide estimates, the percentage of students with disabilities who received all of their PE in a self-contained, adapted PE class ranged from 0 percent to 6 percent.[20] However, some self-contained PE classes may follow the same curriculum as general PE classes. Officials in two schools we visited told us that students with severe disabilities were in self-contained special education classes and took general PE together as a class.

Schools Cited Teacher Preparation and Budget Constraints as Key Challenges to Serving Students with Disabilities in General PE Classes

A notable challenge to serving students with disabilities in general PE classes is the lack of sufficient training or experience among PE or classroom teachers, according to our interviews and other research.[21] Many state, district, and school officials we interviewed said that PE teachers typically take one course on working with students with disabilities in their undergraduate training. This coursework may not always include practical experience working with students with disabilities, and several studies found that PE teachers reported feeling insufficiently prepared to teach students with disabilities.[22] According to SHPPS, only 32 percent of teachers surveyed who taught required PE classes reported having received training on how to work with students with long-term physical, medical, or cognitive disabilities in the 2 years preceding the 2006 study.[23] Officials from several disability, health, or PE associations said that general PE or classroom teachers who lack training or experience teaching students with disabilities may not know what to do or how to provide the appropriate level of accommodations or effectively adapt their instruction. Their lack of training and experience may result in their excusing some students with disabilities from portions of the class, according to two associations we interviewed. Some parents we spoke with described instances in which their children sat on the side during certain activities or were not encouraged to be as active as their classmates. Several parents noted that while PE teachers may not intend to be exclusionary, they were not sufficiently trained on how to include students with disabilities in their classes.

Some state, district, and school officials we interviewed said teachers who teach general PE need more training opportunities regarding students with disabilities, yet resources for training are not always available. Some officials from states and districts said they provide professional development opportunities to teachers through online training, workshops, or conferences. However, budget shortfalls limited their ability to offer additional training opportunities for PE teachers. Some district officials told us that they would like to receive more information on meeting the needs of students with disabilities in general PE settings. For instance, officials from a rural district in Georgia said that they did not have any teachers who specifically taught adapted PE and all students were taught by a general PE or special education teacher. Officials from this district acknowledged that their teachers would benefit from additional training in adapted PE, but told us that they could only provide training if it were available at a low cost or if they had additional resources.

Officials in many of the districts and schools we visited reported that budget constraints created a challenge to providing PE to students with disabilities, particularly in the general PE classroom. For example, many district and school officials, including PE teachers, told us that budget constraints in their schools have resulted in large general PE classes and have hindered teachers' ability to provide students with disabilities the individual attention they may need. In both of the districts in California that we visited, teachers and school officials said that PE classes can include over 45 students, often with only one teacher. Several teachers noted that they would like to provide more individual attention to students with disabilities in their classes but cannot do so while managing the rest of the class. Another PE teacher in Minnesota said that large classes in a spacious and noisy environment can be particularly hard for students with emotional or behavioral disabilities who are very sensitive to such stimuli. District and school officials said that additional staff, such as paraprofessional aides who could work one-on-one with students with disabilities, would help address the challenge of large classes. However, officials said that budget constraints limit the use of aides. Finally, teachers or district officials in several states told us that limited resources for equipment, including special adapted equipment or facility renovations for outdated gymnasiums, hindered their ability to effectively provide opportunities to students with disabilities.

A few state, district, school, and disability association officials we spoke with cited a lack of importance placed on PE as a school subject compared with academic subjects. Some state, district, and school officials noted that the greater emphasis on assessments for reading and math as required by federal law[24] has led them to reduce the number of PE classes that their students are required to take or PE elective courses that they can offer. However, other district officials said their PE offerings have not changed because state laws dictate PE requirements for students, among other reasons.[25] Officials from some districts, schools, disability associations, and parent groups also said that parents of children with disabilities may view PE as a relatively low priority and, subsequently, have low expectations with respect to their children's participation or performance.

SOME STUDENTS WITH DISABILITIES PARTICIPATE IN EXTRACURRICULAR ATHLETICS THROUGH DIFFERENT TYPES OF SCHOOL TEAMS, BUT SCHOOLS FACE CHALLENGES EXPANDING THESE OPPORTUNITIES

Limited Data Suggest That Some Students with Disabilities Participate in School Extracurricular Athletics, but Various Factors May Affect Their Participation

National data show that students with disabilities participate in extracurricular athletics but do not fully distinguish whether these athletic opportunities are offered through schools or out-of-school (i.e., through community-based) programs. According to SEELS estimates, 41 percent of students with disabilities in grades 1 through 7 participated in school or community-based extracurricular athletics in 2000. Additionally, according to NLTS2 estimates, 33 percent of students with disabilities in grades 7 through 12 participated in school or community-based extracurricular athletics in 2001.[26] In these studies, more students with disabilities reported participating in school or community-based sports teams than in other extracurricular activities surveyed, such as performance groups (e.g., band or choir), scouting, or special interest groups (e.g., chess or other hobby clubs).[27] However, sports participation was consistently higher for boys with disabilities than for girls with disabilities across age groups.[28] In addition, according to our interviews with Education officials and researchers, we found no national data that was reliable for our purpose of comparing the participation of students with disabilities to students without disabilities in extracurricular athletics.

Among the schools we visited, we found that IDEA students participated in school-based extracurricular athletics at varying rates, but at a lower rate than their peers without disabilities. The percentage of IDEA students who participated in "traditional" school-based extracurricular athletics (that is, athletics not specially designed for students with disabilities) ranged from 6 to 25 percent among the 11 schools we visited that could provide estimates.[29] In contrast, the percent of non-IDEA students who participated in traditional extracurricular athletics ranged from 18 to 73 percent in these schools (see figure 4). In all cases, the participation rates for IDEA students were lower than for non-IDEA students, ranging from 10 to 56 percentage points lower.

A number of factors may contribute to these differences among schools, such as outreach to students with disabilities, priorities of school officials, and the level of competitiveness among athletic teams. Some schools we visited in Florida and California actively reached out to some students with disabilities in an effort to recruit them for extracurricular athletics. Several of the special education teachers in a California school we visited also coached different sports teams; this dual role enabled them to encourage students with disabilities to participate, according to one official. Additionally, the leadership of school officials may affect students' participation in extracurricular athletics, according to some parents, school officials, and officials from disability groups. One parent of a child with a learning disability in California told us that administrators at her daughter's school recognized that extracurricular athletics was an area where she excelled and wrote into her IEP that she could participate even if her grades did not qualify her. In contrast, the competitiveness of some athletic teams can negatively affect participation among students with disabilities. A district official we spoke with in Texas told us that extracurricular athletics in his district were very competitive and that it was unlikely that many students with disabilities would make these teams. Additionally, one parent told us that she took her daughter who has a neurological disorder out of the school volleyball team because of competitive pressures from other parents and students. Perceptions among students, parents, and schools can also affect student participation in extracurricular athletics, according to a number of officials from schools and disability organizations we interviewed. Specifically, students with disabilities may not perceive themselves as athletic and therefore are reluctant to try out for teams, while parents or schools may resist the idea of students participating due to safety concerns.

Student participation on sports teams varies by disability. In most of the schools we visited, officials told us that students with disabilities who participated in extracurricular athletics often had mild cognitive disabilities or learning disabilities. Additionally, national data from NLTS2 indicates that students with hearing impairments, speech impairments, learning disabilities, or other health impairments reported participating on sports teams at a higher rate compared to students with orthopedic impairments, mental retardation, visual impairments, autism, or multiple disabilities.[30] Many officials from schools and disability associations we interviewed said that students with physical disabilities have fewer opportunities in extracurricular athletics compared to students with cognitive disabilities because fewer programs were designed for them. For example, officials said that while students with learning or cognitive disabilities could participate in traditional sports teams with little to no modifications, students with physical disabilities may not be able to do so. Officials from several schools and disability groups also noted that Special Olympics has had a strong influence nationally in providing opportunities for students with intellectual disabilities but that there is not a similar organization for students with physical disabilities.[31]

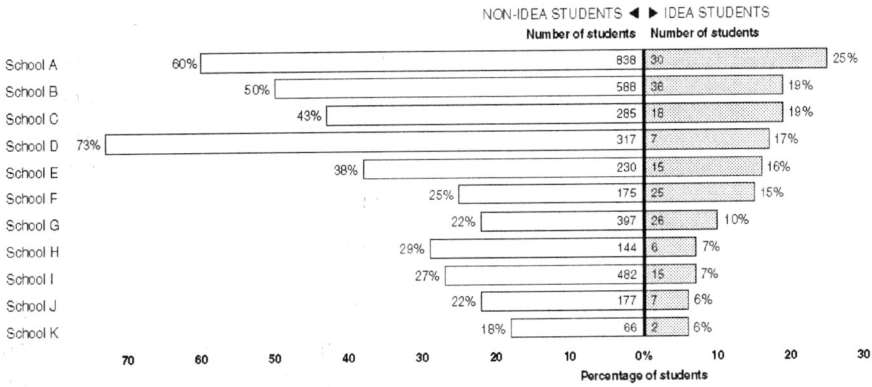

Source: GAO analysis of participation estimates provided by district and school officials.

Notes: Among schools we interviewed, six elementary schools which did not offer formal extracurricular athletic programs and three high schools which could not provide us with data are not included in the figure. Data for each school we visited can be found in table 3 of appendix II.

Figure 4. Percentage of IDEA and Non-IDEA Students Participating in Traditional Extracurricular Athletics in the Schools We Visited

Schools Took Various Steps to Provide Extracurricular Athletic Opportunities to Students with Disabilities

Officials from all 15 districts we spoke with told us that all students in their districts, including those with disabilities, are allowed to try out for their school's interscholastic athletics teams. In addition, many schools we visited said they have at least some teams that accept all students who try out. These teams were usually those based on individual performance, such as track or swimming, according to school officials. In contrast, other teams, such as soccer or basketball, were very competitive and had a limited number of positions available. Many school officials told us that if a student did not get selected to play on a competitive team, they were encouraged by coaches to play on a team that accepted all students.

American Association of Adapted Sports Programs (AAASP)

Source: AAASP, Inc.

Georgia's Department of Education and its state athletic association have a partnership with AAASP to offer adapted sports, such as wheelchair basketball and football. Since 1997, AAASP has helped start programs and train coaches in 24 districts in Georgia. Teams are formed based on student ability, and include students across schools and grades within a district.

School officials reported that they provide varying levels of accommodations for students with disabilities on traditional teams, usually depending on the student's disability. For example, a high school we visited in New Jersey provided an interpreter for a deaf student on the baseball team, and a middle school we visited in California modified rules for deaf and blind students on their wrestling team. State athletic associations in Texas and Minnesota sometimes granted exceptions to their policy on student age limits for students with disabilities.[32] Other methods to aid students with disabilities in extracurricular athletics were less formal. Coaches told us that they may vary their style to meet individual student needs as a practice of good coaching but did not provide any specific accommodations for students with disabilities. For example, coaches in schools that we visited in New Jersey and Florida told us that they repeat rules or give instructions by modeling an activity for students with cognitive or learning disabilities in order to help them better understand game rules.

A few schools provided extracurricular athletic opportunities to students with disabilities through formal partnerships with community programs, most commonly Special Olympics. While many schools provided referrals to Special Olympics but did not otherwise facilitate participation, a few schools we visited provided transportation, coaching, or funds to enable students with intellectual disabilities to participate in Special Olympics. Some of these schools also incorporated Special Olympics coaching and activities into class time for students. In addition, a few schools and districts we visited partnered with other community organizations to provide extracurricular athletic opportunities. In Maryland, one high school we visited collaborated with a local golf club to provide extracurricular golf to students with disabilities and an elementary school partnered with the city's parks and recreation program to provide a sports program for these students.

MINNESOTA ADAPTEDATHLETICS

Source: MnPrepPhoto.com © (2008).

- Since 1992, the Minnesota State High School League has sponsored adapted soccer, floor hockey, and softball.

- More recently, it introduced adapted bowling to address challenges that districts faced regarding the lack of sufficient numbers of students to form a team or great distances between districts that made regular competition difficult. Students go to their local bowling alley to compete "virtually" against students from other schools.
- Across all sports, students with physical impairments and cognitive impairments play on separate teams. Participating students may earn varsity letters.
- About a quarter of the districts in the state offer at least one adapted sports program, according to officials.

Although less common, a few schools we visited offered athletic opportunities to students with disabilities through adapted teams that were overseen by the state athletics association. While students can choose to try out for traditional athletic teams, adapted teams generally target students—such as those with physical or severe cognitive impairments—who may have difficulty participating in traditional teams. Nationally, four states (Georgia, Minnesota, Ohio, and Vermont) offered adapted athletics through their state high school associations in the 2007-2008 school year, according to the NFHS. In addition, state athletic association officials in Maryland, New Jersey, and Florida planned to offer new adapted athletics for students with disabilities in the coming year. Maryland and New Jersey planned to implement these as a result of recent state legislation,[33] as follows:

- Maryland passed the Fitness and Athletics Equity for Students with Disabilities Act in May 2008. Under this new law, the state board and county school systems generally must (1) ensure that students with disabilities have equal opportunity to participate in general ("mainstream") PE and to try out for traditional ("mainstream") athletic programs; (2) provide the reasonable accommodations necessary to allow students with disabilities an opportunity to participate to the fullest extent possible in mainstream PE and athletic programs; and (3) ensure that alternative PE and athletic programs are available, such as adapted sports (only students with disabilities) or unified sports (includes students with and without disabilities). County school systems must develop policies and procedures to promote and protect the inclusion of students with disabilities into mainstream PE and athletic programs and report annually to the State Department of Education. The State Board of Education must adopt a model policy to assist with implementation, while the State Department of Education must monitor compliance and provide technical assistance to county school systems.

- New Jersey passed a much less detailed law in August 2009 that directs the New Jersey State Interscholastic Athletic Association to establish interscholastic adapted athletics for students with visual impairments or physical disabilities who are participating in an adapted athletic program developed by a school district. The New Jersey State Interscholastic Athletic Association must require coaches of adapted athletics to receive training specific to that program but the law does not outline other requirements.

Lack of Information and Budget Constraints May Prevent Schools from Providing More Athletic Opportunities to Students with Disabilities

Officials from several districts and state athletic associations said they generally lacked information that would help them provide extracurricular athletic opportunities for students with disabilities. For instance, a number of district officials said coaches do not receive training specifically on how to work with students with disabilities. Some parents we spoke with said that coaches who do not have such training can be overly focused on winning and fail to fully include students with disabilities on their teams. Other parents noted that coaches are rarely at IEP meetings, and one parent in Minnesota told us that a coach improperly removed her child from a team for being academically ineligible without considering the student's IEP. Additionally, some states and districts lacked information on how to implement new adapted athletic programs for students with disabilities. For example, while the Florida High School Athletic Association planned to initiate a wheelchair track event in the coming year, state and district officials we spoke with said they had questions about how eligibility would be determined and how to provide the equipment needed for these students to participate. Other state athletic associations we interviewed were hesitant to consider offering adapted athletic programs because they did not know how competitive events would be held or how teams would be formed.

Further, some districts lacked information and clarity regarding their responsibilities to provide opportunities under Section 504 for students with disabilities who want to participate in extracurricular athletics equal to those provided to other students. Officials in two districts and several disability associations told us that Education's Section 504 regulations regarding schools' responsibilities to provide extracurricular opportunities are ambiguous. For example, a few disability associations noted that there is lack of clarity regarding how "equal opportunity" should be defined. Officials from another district questioned whether their responsibilities included providing specifically designed programs for students with disabilities, such as separate adapted athletics, particularly within a school environment focused on greater inclusion for students with disabilities.

State, district, and school officials often cited budget constraints as another key challenge to expanding athletic opportunities to all students, including those with disabilities. Officials from seven of the 10 districts we visited said that overall budget constraints have affected funding for their entire athletics program, including funds for personnel and equipment. For example, a rural district we visited in Florida told us that they do not have the resources to fund many personnel positions or buy equipment and that they had to eliminate their athletic director position this year. Another district in California told us that the state's budget situation has negatively impacted all extracurricular athletics and the district is considering dropping their sports teams in the near future. In addition, district officials cited as a concern the high cost of transporting students with disabilities. Officials in one district in Florida noted that transporting students with disabilities was the largest cost in the district's extracurricular athletic program. Some school and district officials we spoke with had concerns about the facilities used for competitions. A district official in Florida noted that many facilities are old and the costs associated with making these fields accessible for students with disabilities would be challenging. Finally, some school officials said that budget limitations for their athletic programs limit their ability to create new adapted teams, due to costs associated with training and maintaining coaches and aides to work with students.

EDUCATION HAS PROVIDED STATES AND SCHOOLS LITTLE SUPPORT REGARDING PE OR ATHLETICS FOR STUDENTS WITH DISABILITIES, AND MANY DISTRICTS WE VISITED SAID MORE WOULD BE USEFUL

Education Has Provided Little Information or Guidance

While OSEP monitors states' implementation of IDEA and provides information, resources, and technical assistance to states and schools on teaching students with disabilities, very little of it is related to PE or extracurricular athletics, according to OSEP officials and our review of Education Web sites. Beyond technical assistance to current or prospective grantees for special education grants, OSEP has not provided any other relevant information or support. OSEP officials said that OSEP has not used its limited resources to provide such information or support because IDEA's monitoring priorities are focused on other areas and the office has not received relevant concerns or complaints from states, schools, or parents.[34]

Similarly, OCR has not widely disseminated any detailed guidance or information on schools' responsibilities to provide opportunities in PE or extracurricular athletics for students with disabilities under Section 504, according to agency officials and our review of OCR's Web site. Based on data from OCR officials, 12,543 complaints were made to its office, from fiscal year 2005 to fiscal year 2009, regarding elementary and secondary school students with disabilities. Of these, 108 of the complaints filed between fiscal year 2005 and fiscal year 2009 (less than 1 percent) pertained to discrimination regarding student participation in PE or extracurricular athletics. From these 108 complaints, we reviewed a subset of 20 and found that 16 alleged that a student was denied equal opportunity to participate in extracurricular athletics.[35] When resolving a Section 504 complaint investigation, OCR may provide detailed guidance or training to help individual districts or schools meet their responsibilities regarding PE or athletics. However, according to OCR officials, such guidance is tailored to the needs of the district or school based on facts obtained through an OCR investigation, and OCR has not yet issued guidance specifically on Section 504's requirements concerning PE or athletics. Our review of OCR guidance found several documents that state that students with disabilities may not be excluded on the basis of a disability from an extracurricular activity, which may include athletics, and that students must be provided opportunities to participate in these activities equal to those of other students. However, with regard to PE and extracurricular athletics, these documents do not provide information beyond what is stated in the Section 504 regulations. In contrast, OCR has provided more detailed guidance in other civil rights areas, such as letters, pamphlets, and question and answer sheets.[36] OCR officials said they have not yet issued additional guidance on extracurricular athletic opportunities for students with disabilities in part due to resource constraints and their focus on other areas of civil rights, such as gender discrimination in athletics or harassment based on race, sex, and disability. They also noted that these areas have received more official complaints and persistent concerns from constituents such as parents and community groups.

Through several grant programs, Education has administered a relatively small amount of funds specifically to support PE or extracurricular athletic opportunities for students with disabilities. For example, OSEP administers a grant program that provides funding to institutes of higher education for the development of special education personnel. In fiscal year 2009, of the $91 million administered for these grants, about 2 percent was used to support programs intended to provide undergraduate or graduate training in the area of adapted PE. In the same fiscal year, OSEP also administered about $8 million, as specifically directed by Congress, to support Special Olympics programs. These federal funds are administered under the Special Olympics Sport and Empowerment Act of 2004 and are intended to increase the participation of individuals with intellectual disabilities in sports and competitive activities. They are also used to design and implement Special Olympics education programs that can be integrated into classroom instruction. In addition, the Office of Safe and Drug-Free Schools (OSDFS) administers the Carol M. White Physical Education Program—the only dedicated PE program sponsored by Education. However, according to OSDFS officials, less than 1 percent of the program's overall funding of $77 million in fiscal year 2009 was used to serve the specific needs of students with disabilities.[37] To serve these needs, grantees used funds to purchase specialized equipment or provide training to teachers and staff on how to adapt their general PE programming and activities for students with disabilities.[38]

Some State and District Officials We Interviewed Said More Information and Guidance Would Be Useful

Officials from several states and many districts we interviewed said that they could benefit from Education helping states and schools share relevant information, such as practices or resources regarding PE and extracurricular athletics for students with disabilities. For example, officials from one state told us that when they recently developed new guidance for schools in PE and extracurricular athletics for students with disabilities, they could have benefited from information on what other states were doing in these areas. Officials from another state noted that Education could collect information on promising practices and share these with institutes of higher education that offer PE teacher training programs. Additionally, officials from 14 out of 15 districts we interviewed indicated that additional information or resources from Education on how to offer PE or extracurricular athletic opportunities to students with disabilities would be useful. For example, an adapted PE coordinator in a California district said that while he draws on existing informational resources, such as private sector Web sites[39] and state or local conferences, he is constantly looking for additional information from others in his field on good practices and policies. Similarly, a PE and health director in a Florida district noted that as more states implement new wheelchair track and field activities in the general high school athletic program, supporting information and procedural practices would be helpful.

Further, a number of officials from various associations we interviewed, including those representing special education, PE, and adapted sports, said that Education should share information on successful practices or provide informational resources such as factsheets or toolkits. Some association officials also said that Education could give additional attention to PE or extracurricular athletics, by providing information online or promoting greater awareness through media campaigns. This attention would increase awareness among schools about the types of opportunities that could be provided, promote interest among students with disabilities to participate in such activities, and address concerns and questions among parents.

Officials from many districts and several disability groups also said that additional guidance from Education, specifically on extracurricular athletics, would be useful. Officials in 12 of 15 districts we spoke with told us that additional clarification and communication from Education regarding schools' responsibilities under Section 504 in providing extracurricular athletics to students with disabilities would be useful. Specifically, one district official noted that the lack of clarity in federal requirements regarding how schools should define and provide equal opportunities serves as a disincentive for schools to take proactive steps to provide additional opportunities for students with disabilities. Another said that while most districts give a "good faith effort" to provide equal opportunities in extracurricular activities, including athletics, district officials probably do not fully understand what it means to provide equal opportunities until a problem arises, such as parent concerns or complaints. According to this official, districts would benefit from additional information on the legal issues or processes involved in allowing students with disabilities to participate in extracurricular athletics, as well as how to document instances in which a student is or is not allowed to participate. Officials from another district noted that school responsibilities related to special education services or supports for activities that occurred after school, such as extracurricular athletics, as opposed to those during the school day, were not entirely clear. Similarly, officials from several disability groups noted that OCR could do more to ensure that schools provide equal opportunities in extracurricular athletics, such as by reminding schools of their responsibilities and what they entail (e.g., through informational factsheets). Officials from one disability association also said that they do not believe parents and students with disabilities know where to turn for help with respect to problems regarding extracurricular athletics and that OCR could help inform parents and schools by issuing a letter reminding them that OCR is a resource.

CONCLUSIONS

All students, including those with disabilities, benefit from the positive effects that physical activity and school athletics have on an individual's health, social well-being, and self-esteem. While available data show that students with disabilities generally are participating in physical education classes to a similar extent as students without disabilities and that some also are involved in school sports, we found that many districts and schools we visited are interested in improving how they provide physical education and athletic opportunities to these students. Garnering additional resources to provide such opportunities is difficult at a time when states and districts are operating under severe fiscal constraints. However, certain districts and schools may have developed approaches or activities to engage students with disabilities more fully in the PE classroom or in extracurricular athletics, and leveraging their expertise could be helpful to other schools that face challenges in these areas. Some schools may also be uncertain about their exact responsibilities to provide opportunities to students with disabilities equal to those of other students, particularly regarding extracurricular athletics. Without additional clarification from Education, schools may not be providing some students full access to these opportunities. While Education has not addressed these issues because it has targeted its limited resources to other areas, focusing some of its existing resources on helping schools provide opportunities in PE and extracurricular athletics could yield important benefits and enable students with disabilities to more fully experience the rewards of physical activity.

Recommendations for Executive Action

To help states and schools access existing knowledge and resources, we recommend that the Secretary of Education facilitate information sharing among states and schools on ways to provide opportunities in PE and extracurricular athletics to students with disabilities. For instance, Education could provide Web site links to resources or practices used by states, districts, schools, or organizations in PE or extracurricular athletics for students with disabilities. Such information could be posted on its Web site or discussed at conferences or Webinars.

To ensure that schools are aware of their responsibilities and that students with disabilities consistently have opportunities to participate in extracurricular athletics equal to those of other students, we recommend that Education clarify and communicate schools' responsibilities under Section 504 of the Rehabilitation Act regarding the provision of extracurricular athletics. For example, Education could provide clarifying guidance to schools through its Web site or at conferences.

Appendix I. Scope and Methodology

To address the objectives of this study, we used a variety of methods. Specifically, we

- examined pertinent data from four nationally representative studies;

- conducted site visits in five states and phone interviews with two additional states;
- conducted 21 interviews with representatives from national associations, community organizations, parent advocacy centers, or researchers in the areas of disability, health, physical education (PE), special education, and athletics; and
- interviewed officials from the Department of Education (Education) about Education's oversight and technical assistance efforts, and reviewed relevant federal laws, regulations, guidance, and other agency documentation and data pertaining to PE and extracurricular athletics for students with disabilities.[40]

National Datasets

To obtain national information on the extent to which schools provide students with disabilities opportunities in PE and extracurricular athletics, we identified four nationally representative studies with the most recent data available for our purposes. Specifically, we examined pertinent data from the 2005 Youth Risk Behavior Survey (YRBS) and cited published data from the 2006 School Health Policies and Programs Study (SHPPS).[41] Both studies are administered by the Department of Health and Human Services' Centers for Disease Control and Prevention. YRBS surveys students in grades 9 through 12 on health-risk behaviors, and SHPPS collects survey information on school health programs and practices from state, district, and school officials, as well as teachers and parents. We also examined 2001 data from Education's National Longitudinal Transition Study-2 (NLTS2) and 2000 data from Education's Special Education Elementary Longitudinal Study (SEELS). To calculate the percentage of students with disabilities in these studies who did not participate in sports, we included students who reported not participating in any extracurricular activities, as well as students who reported participating in some extracurricular activities but not sports. SEELS and NLTS2 consist of nationally representative samples of students who received special education services. Students in SEELS were 6 to 12 years old and in at least the first grade in 1999, and students in NLTS2 were 13 to 16 years old and in at least the seventh grade in 2000 (see table 2).

Table 2. National Studies We Examined That Contain Data about Students with Disabilities in PE and Extracurricular Athletics

Study	Funding agency	Year	Focus	Groups surveyed	Definition of disability	Web site as of 4/7/2010
Department of Education						
Special Education Elementary Longitudinal Study (SEELS)	Office of Special Education Programs	2000[a]	Experience of students with disabilities transitioning from elementary and middle school to middle and high school	Students with disabilities, parents, teachers, and school administrators	Student is receiving special education services (has a disability covered by IDEA)	http://www.seels.net/grindex.html
National Longitudinal Transition Study-2 (NLTS2)	National Center for Special Education Research	2001[b]	Experience of students with disabilities trans-itioning from secondary school into early adulthood	Students with disabilities, parents, teachers, and School Administrators	Student is receiving special education services (has a disability covered by IDEA)	http://www.nlts2.org/index.html
Centers for Disease Control and Prevention						
School Health Policies and Programs Study (SHPPS)	Division of Adole-scent and School Health, National Center for Chronic	2006	Components of school health policies and programs, including physical	State, district, and school officials, and health and physical education teachers	Survey asks about policies and practices related to students with long-term	http://www.cdc.gov/HealthyYouth/SHPPS/

Table 2. (Continued)

Study	Funding agency	Year	Focus	Groups surveyed	Definition of disability	Web site as of 4/7/2010
	Disease Prevent-ion and Health Promotion		education and activity		physical, medical, or cognitive disabilities	
Youth Risk Behavior Survey (YRBS)	Division of Adol-escent and School Health, National Center for Chronic Disease Prevention and Health Promotion	2005[c]	Health-risk behaviors and prevalence of obesity and asthma among youth and young adults	Students in grades 9-12 with and without disabilities	Survey asks students if they have any physical disabilities or long-term health problems	http://www.cdc.gov/HealthyYouth/yrbs/index.htm

Source: GAO.

[a] SEELS data were collected between 1999 and 2004. This report uses the first wave of data, which were collected in 2000.

[b] NLTS2 data were collected between 2000 and 2009. This report uses the first wave of data, which were collected in 2001.

[c] YRBS is conducted every 2 years. YRBS was conducted in 2007 and 2009, but 2005 is the only year that student respondents were asked whether they had a disability.

We selected these sources, in consultation with GAO methodologists, because they contained nationally representative information about the participation of students with disabilities in PE and extracurricular athletics and were determined to be sufficiently reliable for the purposes of our report. We examined the studies' technical documentation to determine their purpose, the population described, the sample surveyed, data collection methods, and the focus of questions and variables related to students with disabilities and PE and extracurricular athletics. Using this documentation, and through interviews with knowledgeable agency officials, we evaluated the reliability and quality of these data, as well as the extent to which they could be used to answer our questions. Additionally, while more recent data are available from NLTS2 and SEELS, we determined, through interviews with knowledgeable agency officials and our own analyses, that the data collected during the first wave of these two longitudinal studies were preferable, for substantive and technical reasons, for the purposes of our report. Such substantive issues included relevant student grade levels, and technical reasons included high attrition rates in later waves. We used the same methodology as Education to produce estimates on the participation in extracurricular athletics among students with disabilities. We determined that the data we analyzed were sufficiently reliable for our purposes.

We assessed the quality, reliability, and usability of the data for reporting descriptive statistics on the demographic characteristics of students with disabilities (e.g., grade level, gender, and type of disability), and their participation in PE and extracurricular athletics. Because each of the three surveys we provided estimates for (SEELS, NLTS2, and YRBS) followed a selection procedure based on random selections, each sample is only one of a number of samples that might have been drawn.[42] To assess the precision of estimates from these three surveys, we calculated confidence intervals at the 95 percent level for each measure. A confidence interval gives an estimated range of values, calculated from sample data, which is likely to include the true measure of the population.[43] All percentage estimates from SEELS and NLTS2 used in this report have 95 percent confidence intervals within plus or minus 4 percentage points, unless otherwise noted. All percentage estimates from YRBS used in this report have 95 percent confidence intervals within plus or minus 7 percentage points, unless otherwise noted. All SHPPS estimates have 95 percent confidence intervals within plus or minus 5.5 percentage points of the estimates, unless otherwise noted. All comparisons made between groups are significant, unless otherwise noted. We analyzed data from YRBS, SEELS, and NLTS2 using SUDAAN (Survey Data

Analysis)®,[44] a statistical analysis software package with capabilities to analyze surveys with a stratified, multistaged cluster sampling design, such as that found in YRBS, SEELS, and NLTS2.

Site Visits

To address all three of our objectives, we conducted site visits in five states (California, Florida, Maryland, Minnesota, and New Jersey) and interviewed officials from state departments of education, state athletic associations, school districts, and schools. We also interviewed teachers, coaches, parents, and students. In each of these states we visited two school districts and four schools. In addition, we conducted phone interviews with officials from state agencies and two to three school district offices in Georgia and Texas. We selected these seven states because they were in the top half of states in numbers of both IDEA students and Section 504 students and varied in whether they had policies requiring elementary, middle, and secondary schools to teach PE, and geographic location.[45] We chose school districts that provided variation in their percentages of students with disabilities, socio-economic status,[46] and classification as urban, rural, or suburban. In deciding between multiple states or districts that met our selection criteria, we purposely chose some that external stakeholders recommended as having innovative or promising practices. We spoke with parents by contacting one to two Parent Training and Information Centers in each state we visited.[47] These parent centers are funded by Education and provide information and support to families of children with disabilities of all ages. For this study, staff from these centers asked parent members to voluntarily meet with GAO to share their children's experiences in PE and extracurricular athletics. At some meetings, children also attended with their parents and shared their views. We cannot generalize to all states, school districts, or schools based on these site visits.

Through our site visits and phone interviews, we gathered information on relevant state and district policies, available data or estimates on students' participation in PE and extracurricular athletics, and factors that may affect participation. We also inquired about the approaches districts and schools use to provide opportunities in PE and extracurricular athletics, key challenges to providing these opportunities, and areas in which federal assistance has been or would be useful. When possible, we reviewed written documentation and policies from state agencies, districts, and schools. We also observed some classrooms and athletic practices and spoke with groups of students at schools we visited. To enhance the consistency of the information we obtained from interviews, we used structured sets of questions for officials from state agencies, district offices, and schools, as well as parents. We analyzed interview information by developing and testing a coding structure and coding the interviews using NVivo, a qualitative analysis software. One team member coded all the interviews, and another reviewed 100 percent of the coded output for accuracy.

APPENDIX II. STUDENT PARTICIPATION IN PHYSICAL EDUCATION AND EXTRACURRICULARATHLETICS IN DISTRICT AND SCHOOLS WE VISITED

Using a short questionnaire, we obtained estimates from officials in the districts and schools we visited of the number of students with disabilities in PE and extracurricular athletics. We inquired about students covered under IDEA, as well as those covered under Section 504, but not IDEA. However, we did not include numbers of students covered only under Section 504 in these tables due to the number of missing responses and the few students in each district or school in this group. We visited two schools in each district we visited.

Table 3. IDEA Student Participation in PE among Schools and Districts Visited

	Total student enrollment	Total IDEA students	IDEA students in general PE with no accommodations or modifications		IDEA students in general PE with some accommodations or modifications		IDEA students who receive adapted PE		IDEA students exempt from PE	
			Number	Percent	Number	Percent	Number	Percent	Number	Percent
Districts										
District 1	82,260	13,908	7,674	55%	13	0%	296	2%	0	0%
District 2	2,747	341	333	98	0	0	8	2	0	0
District 3	14,381	1,626	1,391	86	6	0	105	6	0	0
District 4	19,094	2,600	2,400	92	200	8	58	2	x	x
District 5	6,458	856	598	70	77	9	156	18	1	0.1
District6	49,138	4,609	x	x	x	x	422	9	0	0
District 7	345,458	38,339	x	x	x	x	x	x	x	x
District 8	39,481	7,058	6,658	94	400	6	0	0	0	0
District 9	4,320	569	x	x	x	x	57	10	0	0
District 10	30,385	4,171	x	x	x	x	91	2	1	0.02
Schools										
School A	1,506	120	103	86	10	8	4	3	0	0
School B	1,368	188	x	x	x	x	15	8	0	0
School C	765	97	94	97	0	0	2	2	0	0
School D	474	41	13	32	13	32	0	0	1	2
School E	694	92	90	98	0	0	2	2	0	0
School F	855	166	133	80	33	20	22	13	0	0
School G	2,017	248	243	98	0	0	5	2	0	0
School H	582	83	67	81	16	19	16	19	0	0

Table 3. (Continued)

	Total student enrollment	Total IDEA students	IDEA students in general PE with no accommodations or modifications		IDEA students in general PE with some accommodations or modifications		IDEA students who receive adapted PE		IDEA students exempt from PE	
			Number	Percent	Number	Percent	Number	Percent	Number	Percent
School I	2,046	228	29	13	0	0	28	12	x	x
School J	903	110	50	45	1	1	32	29	1	1
School K	401	31	31	100	0	0	0	0	0	0
School L	1,652	327	327	100	0	0	0	0	0	0
School M	1,978	298	200	67	10	3	20	7	x	x
School N	1,683	159	146	92	x	x	13	8	x	x
School O	522	63	0	0	63	100	0	0	0	0
School P	747	90	89	99	1	1	0	0	0	0
School Q	735	72	65	90	13	18	4	6	0	0
School R	474	69	68	98	1	2	0	0	0	0
School S	461	79	x	x	x	x	15	19	0	0
School T	478	54	54	100	0	0	0	0	0	0

Source: Participation estimates provided by district and school officials we interviewed.

Notes: Some students may not have been enrolled in PE in the semester we visited, and the number of students in the individual categories may not equal the total number of IDEA students.

X means "don't know" or no response was provided.

Table 4. IDEA and Non-IDEA Student Participation in School-Based Traditional Extracurricular Athletics among Districts and Schools Visited

	Students covered under IDEA			Students not covered under IDEA		
	Total students	**Number who participate in traditional extracurricular athletics**	**Percent of total who participate in traditional extracurricular athletics**	**Total students**	**Number who participate in traditional extracurricular athletics**	**Percent of total who participate in traditional extracurricular athletics**
Districts						
District 1	**13,908**	x	x	**68,352**	x	x
District 2	**341**	33	10%	**2,406**	515	21%
District 3	**1,626**	47	3	**12,755**	701	5
District 4	**2,600**	x	x	**16,494**	x	x
District 5	**856**	36	4	**5,602**	376	7
District 6	**4,609**	263	6	**44,529**	9,686	22
District 7	**38,339**	x	x	**307,119**	x	x
District 8	**7,058**	x	x	**32,423**	x	x
District 9	**569**	36	6	**3,751**	588	16
District 10	**4,171**	x	x	**26,214**	x	x
Schools						
School A	**120**	30	25	**1,386**	838	60
School B	**188**	36	19	**1,180**	588	50
School C	**97**	18	19	**668**	285	43
School D	**41**	7	17	**433**	317	73
School E	**92**	15	16	**602**	230	38
School F	**166**	25	15	**689**	175	25
School G	**248**	26	10	**1,769**	397	22

Table 4. (Continued)

	Students covered under IDEA			Students not covered under IDEA		
	Total students	**Number who participate in traditional extracurricular athletics**	**Percent of total who participate in traditional extracurricular athletics**	**Total students**	**Number who participate in traditional extracurricular athletics**	**Percent of total who participate in traditional extracurricular athletics**
School H	**83**	6	7	**499**	144	29
School I	**228**	15	7	**1,818**	482	27
School J	**110**	7	6	**793**	177	22
School K	**31**	2	6	**370**	66	18
School L	**327**	x	x	**1,325**	x	x
School M	**298**	60	20	**1,680**	x	x
School N	**159**	x	x	**1,524**	x	x

Source: Participation estimates provided by district and school officials we interviewed.

Notes: Our questionnaire asked districts and schools specifically about "regular extracurricular interscholastic sports" to distinguish between sports that are designed specifically for students with disabilities.

Six elementary schools we interviewed did not offer formal extracurricular athletic programs and are not included in the table.

X means "don't know" or no response was provided.

APPENDIX III. NATIONAL DATA ON STUDENT PARTICIPATION IN PHYSICAL EDUCATION AND EXTRACURRICULAR ATHLETICS

Unless otherwise noted, differences made between groups in these tables are not statistically significant at p-value less than 0.05.

Table 5. Population Estimates: Number of Days per Week Students with and without Disabilities Attend PE Class

	Students with physical disabilities or long-term health problems	Students without physical disabilities or long-term health problems
0 days	48%	47%
1 day	2	2
2 days	5	3
3 days	12	12
4 days	3	3
5 days	29	34

Source: GAO analysis of YRBS, 2005.

Note: Estimates may not add to 100 percent due to rounding.

Table 6. Population Estimates: Number of Days per Week Girls and Boys with Disabilities Attend PE Class

	Girls with physical disabilities or long-term health problems	Boys with physical disabilities or long-term health problems
0 days	54%	39%
1 day	1	2
2 days	6	4
3 days	12	12
4 days	2	5
5 days	24	37

Source: GAO analysis of YRBS, 2005.

Note: Estimates may not add to 100 percent due to rounding.

Table 7. Population Estimates: Number of Days per Week Girls with and without Disabilities Attend PE Class

	Girls with physical disabilities or long-term health problems	Girls without physical disabilities or long-term health problems
0 days	54%	53%
1 day	1	1
2 days	6	3
3 days	12	11
4 days	2	2
5 days	24	30

Source: GAO analysis of YRBS, 2005.

Note: Estimates may not add to 100 percent due to rounding.

Table 8. Population Estimates: Number of Days per Week Boys with and without Disabilities Attend PE Class

	Boys With Physical Disabilities or Long-Term Health Problems	Boys Without Physical Disabilities or Long-Term Health Problems
0 days	39%	41%
1 day	2	2
2 days	4	3
3 days	12	13
4 days	5	4
5 days	37	37

Source: GAO analysis of YRBS, 2005.

Note: Estimates may not add to 100 percent due to rounding.

Table 9. Population Estimates: Percentage of Students who Actually Played Sports or Exercised in a Typical PE Class

	Students with Physical Disabilities or Long-Term Health Problems	Students without Physical Disabilities or Long-Term Health Problems
Less than 10 minutes	3%	3%
10 to 20 minutes	4	5
21 to 30 minutes	10	8

Table 9. (Continued)

	Students with Physical Disabilities or Long-Term Health Problems	Students without Physical Disabilities or Long-Term Health Problems
31 to 40 minutes	10	11
41 to 50 minutes	8	9
51 to 60 minutes	6	6
More than 60 minutes	10	12

Source: GAO analysis of YRBS, 2005.

Table10. Population Estimates: Percentage of Girls and Boys with Disabilities who Actually Played Sports or Exercised in a Typical PE Class

	Girls with Physical Disabilities or Long-Term Health Problems	Boys with Physical Disabilities or Long-Term Health Problems
Less than 10 minutes	3%	4%
10 to 20 minutes	5	4
21 to 30 minutes	10	10
31 to 40 minutes[a]	6	16
41 to 50 minutes	7	10
51 to 60 minutes	5	7
More than 60 minutes	9	12

Source: GAO analysis of YRBS, 2005.

[a] Differences between girls and boys with physical disabilities or long-term health problems are statistically significant at p-value less than 0.05.

Table 11. Population Estimates: Percentage of Girls with and without Disabilities who Actually Played Sports or Exercised in a Typical PE Class

	Girls with physical disabilities or long-term health problems	Girls without physical disabilities or long-term health problems
Less than 10 minutes	3%	3%
10 to 20 minutes	5	5
21 to 30 minutes	10	9

Table 11. (Continued)

	Girls with physical disabilities or long-term health problems	Girls without physical disabilities or long-term health problems
31 to 40 minutes	6	10
41 to 50 minutes	7	8
51 to 60 minutes	5	5
More than 60 minutes	9	8

Source: GAO analysis of YRBS, 2005.

Table 12. Population Estimates: Percentage of Boys with and without Disabilities who Actually Played Sports or Exercised in a Typical PE Class

	Boys with physical disabilities or long-term health problems	Boys without physical disabilities or long-term health problems
Less than 10 minutes	4%	2%
10 to 20 minutes	4	5
21 to 30 minutes	10	8
31 to 40 minutes	16	11
41 to 50 minutes	10	11
51 to 60 minutes	7	8
More than 60 minutes	12	15

Source: GAO analysis of YRBS, 2005.

Table 13. Population Estimates: Instructional Settings for Physical Education, Students with Disabilities in Grades 1 through 7 (Ages 6 to 12 at Outset of Study)

	Total students	Grades 1-5	Grades 6-7
General education classrooma	92%	89%	96%
Resource room	4	6	1
Special education self-contained classroom	6	6	4

Source: GAO analysis of SEELS 2000, Wave 1.

Notes: Among students who received PE

Estimates may add up to more than 100 percent because some students may take PE in multiple settings.

[a] Differences between grades 1through 5 and 6 through 8 are statistically significant at p-value less than 0.05.

Table 14. Population Estimates: Instructional Settings for Physical Education, Students with Disabilities in Grades 7 through 12 (Ages 13 to16 at Outset of Study)

	Total students	Grades 7-8	Grades 9-12
General education classroom	88%	92%	84%
Special education self-contained classroom	13	8	16
Individual instruction	0	0	1
Community setting/ different school	1	0	1

Source: GAO analysis of NLTS2 2001, Wave 1.

Notes: Among students who received PE

Estimates may add up to more than 100 percent because some students may take PE in multiple settings.

Table 15. Population Estimates: Participated in a Sports Team, Students with Disabilities in Grades 1 through 7 (Ages 6 to12 at Outset of Study)

	Participated in a sports team	Did not participate in a sports team
Total[a]	**41%**	**59%[b]**
Among Students who Participated in Extracurricular Activities[c]		
School activity only	53	47
Out-of-school activity only	53	47
Both school and out-of-school activity[a]	80	20

Source: GAO analysis of SEELS 2000, Wave 1.

Note: It is not possible to determine whether students who reported participating in a sports team and participating in both in-school and out-of-school extracurricular activities participated in a school-based sports team or a community-based sports team.

[a] Differences between students who participated in a sports team and did not participate in a sports team are statistically significant at p-value less than 0.05.

[b] This includes students who reported participation in no extracurricular activities, but were not asked the follow-up question about sports participation.

[c] To calculate the percentage of students with disabilities in these studies who did not participate in sports, we included students who reported not participating in any

extracurricular activity, as well as students who reported participating in some extracurricular activity but not sports.

Table 16. Population Estimates: Participated in a Sports Team, Students With Disabilities in Grades 7 through 12 (Ages 13 to 16 at Outset of Study)

	Participated in a sports team	Did not participate in a sports team
Total[a]	**33%**	**67%[b]**
Among Students who Participated in Extracurricular Activities[c]		
School activity only	53	47
Out-of-school activity only[a]	31	69
Both school and out-of-school activity[a]	62	38

Source: GAO analysis of NLTS2 2001, Wave 1.

Notes: It is not possible to determine whether students who reported participating in a sports team and participating in both in-school and out-of-school extracurricular activities belonged to a school-based sports team or a community-based sports team.

[a] Differences between students who participated in a sports team and did not participate in a sports team are statistically significant at p-value less than 0.05.

[b] This includes students who reported participation in no extracurricular activities, but were not asked the follow-up question about sports participation.

[c] To calculate the percentage of students with disabilities in these studies who did not participate in sports, we included students who reported not participating in any extracurricular activity, as well as students who reported participating in some extracurricular activity but not sports

Table 17. Population Estimates: Participated in a Sports Team, Students with Disabilities in Grades 1 through 7 (Ages 6 to 12 at Outset of Study), By Gender

	Girls	Boys
Total[a]	**31%**	**45%[b]**
Among Students who Participated in Extracurricular Activities[c]		
School activity only[a]	40	62
Out-of-school activity only[a]	43	58
Both School and out-of-school activity[a]	67	85

Source: GAO analysis of SEELS 2000, Wave 1.

Note: It is not possible to determine whether students who reported participating in a sports team and participating in both in-school and out-of-school extracurricular activities belonged to a school-based sports team or a community-based sports team.

[a] Differences between students who participated in a sports team and did not participate in a sports team are statistically significant at p-value less than 0.05.

[b] This includes students who reported participation in no extracurricular activities, but were not asked the follow-up question about sports participation.

[c] To calculate the percentage of students with disabilities in these studies who did not participate in sports, we included students who reported not participating in any extracurricular activity, as well as students who reported participating in some extracurricular activity but not sports

Table 18. Population Estimates: Participated In a Sports Team, Students With Disabilities in Grades 7 through 12 (Ages 13 to 16 at Outset of Study), by Gender

	Girls	Boys
Total[a]	**23%**	**37%[b]**
Among Students who Participated in Extracurricular Activities[c]		
School activity only[a]	38	58
Out-of-school activity only[a]	18	38
Both School and out-of-school activity[a]	47	69

Source: GAO analysis of NLTS2 2001, Wave 1.

Note: It is not possible to determine whether students who reported participating in a sports team and participating in both in-school and out-of-school extracurricular activities belonged to a school-based sports team or a community-based sports team.

[a] Differences between students who participated in a sports team and did not participate in a sports team are statistically significant at p-value less than 0.05.

[b] This includes students who reported participation in no extracurricular activities, but were not asked the follow-up question about sports participation.

[c] To calculate the percentage of students with disabilities in these studies who did not participate in sports, we included students who reported not participating in any extracurricular activity, as well as students who reported participating in some extracurricular activity but not sports

Table 19. Population Estimates: Participated in a Sports Team, Students with Disabilities in Grades 7 through 12 (Ages 13 to 16 at Outset of Study), by Disability Type

	Participated in a sports team
Hearing impairment	47%
Speech impairment	41
Other health impairment[a]	36
Learning disability[a]	36
Deaf/blindness[a]	27
Traumatic braininjury[a]	27
Visual impairment[a]	25
Emotional disturbance[a]	24
Mental retardation[a]	22
Multiple disabilities[a]	21
Orthopedic impairment[a]	19
Autism[a]	16

Source: GAO analysis of NLTS2 2001, Wave 1.

Notes: These data do not fully distinguish if these athletic opportunities are offered through schools or community programs. It is not possible to determine whether students who reported participating in a sports team and participating in both in-school and out-of-school extracurricular activities belonged to a school-based sports team or a community-based sports team.

[a] Students with hearing impairments participate in sports teams at higher rates compared to students with these types of disabilities and these differences are statistically significant at p-value less than 0.05.

APPENDIX IV. COMMENTS FROM THE DEPARTMENT OF EDUCATION

UNITED STATES DEPARTMENT OF EDUCATION

WASHINGTON, DC 20202-

June 4, 2010

Ms. Cornelia M. Ashby
Director
Education, Workforce, and Income Security Issues
U.S. Government Accountability Office
441 G Street, N.W.
Washington, D.C. 20548

Dear Ms. Ashby:

Thank you for the opportunity to review the draft Government Accountability Office (GAO) report: *Students with Disabilities: More Information and Guidance Could Improve Opportunities in Physical Education and Athletics* (GAO-10-519), and respond on behalf of the Department.

The draft report contains two recommendations for Executive Action, and we outline each recommendation and our responses below.

Recommendation: To help states and schools access existing knowledge and resources, we recommend that the Secretary of Education facilitate information sharing among states and schools on ways to provide opportunities in Physical Education (PE) and extracurricular athletics to students with disabilities. For instance, Education could provide website links to resources or practices used by states, districts, schools, or organizations in PE or extracurricular athletics for students with disabilities. Such information could be posted on its website or discussed at conferences or webinars.

Response: The Department generally agrees with the recommendation, and agrees that further information sharing on providing opportunities in PE and extracurricular athletics to students with disabilities would be helpful to states, schools, and the students. The Department's Office of Special Education and Rehabilitative Services, through the Office of Special Education Programs, working in conjunction with other offices in the Department, will identify useful information on this subject and share that information by posting it on the Department's ed.gov Web site. This information may also be discussed by Department personnel at conferences or in webinars.

Recommendation: To ensure that schools are aware of their responsibilities and that students with disabilities consistently have opportunities to participate in extracurricular athletics equal to those of other students, we recommend that Education clarify and communicate schools' responsibilities under Section 504 of the Rehabilitation Act regarding the provision of extracurricular athletics. For example, Education could provide clarifying guidance to schools through its website or at conferences.

Response: The Department agrees that it is important for schools to be aware of their responsibilities and that students with disabilities have opportunities to participate in extracurricular athletics equal to those of other students. In fiscal year 2011, the Department's Office for Civil Rights intends to issue additional guidance on Section 504 of the Rehabilitation Act and recipients' obligations to provide students with disabilities equal access to extracurricular athletics.

The Department will also provide some technical comments on the report. We appreciate the opportunity to comment on these important matters.

Sincerely,

Alexa Posny, Ph.D.
Assistant Secretary for the
Office of Special Education and Rehabilitative Services

Russlynn Ali
Assistant Secretary for Civil Rights

End Notes

[1] For example, see James H. Rimmer, Jennifer L. Rowland, and Kiyoshi Yamaki, "Obesity and Secondary Conditions in Adolescents with Disabilities: Addressing the Needs of an Underserved Population," *Journal of Adolescent Health*, vol. 41 (2007): 224-229.

[2] For example, see Nancy A. Murphy et al., "Promoting the Participation of Children with Disabilities in Sports, Recreation, and Physical Activities," *Pediatrics*, vol. 121 (2008): 1057-1061 and Coreen M. Harada and Gary N. Siperstein, "The Sport Experience of Athletes with Intellectual Disabilities: A National Survey of Special Olympics Athletes and Their Families," *Adapted Physical Activity Quarterly*, vol. 26 (2009): 68-85.

[3] In this report, we define extracurricular athletics as voluntary sports activities that fall outside the required school curriculum. Our focus is on extracurricular athletics that are school-based, such as soccer or track teams which compete against other schools.

[4] 20 U.S.C. § 1400 et seq.

[5] 29 U.S.C. § 794.

[6] Individuals with disabilities are also protected under the Americans with Disabilities Act of 1990 (ADA), Pub. L. No. 101-336 (1990); 42 U.S.C. § 12101 et seq. For the purposes of Section 504, the Rehabilitation Act defines individuals with disabilities identically to the ADA, and for students in elementary and secondary schools, the U.S. Department of Education interprets the ADA and Section 504 similarly.

[7] Extracurricular activities may also include other recreational activities or special interest groups or clubs.

[8] YRBS and SHPPS are national surveys conducted by the Department of Health and Human Services' Centers for Disease Control and Prevention. YRBS surveys students in grades 9-12 on health-risk behaviors, while SHPPS collects survey information on school health

programs and practices from state, district, and school officials, as well as teachers and parents. SEELS and NLTS2 are longitudinal studies funded by Education and consist of nationally representative samples of students who received special education services. Students in SEELS were 6 to 12 years old in at least the first grade in 1999, and students in NLTS2 were 13 to 16 years old and at least in the 7th grade in 2000.

[9] We obtained information on states' PE requirements from SHPPS.

[10] For data on student enrollment, see Table 52 in Snyder, T.D., and Dillow, S.A. (2010). *Digest of Education Statistics 2009* (NCES 2010-013). National Center for Education Statistics, Institute of Education Sciences, U.S. Department of Education. Washington, D.C. For data on the amount of federal funding, see Office of Special Education Programs' fiscal year 2007 IDEA Part B State Allocation Table, Section 611.

[11] These conditions may be covered under IDEA in some circumstances under the "other health impairment" category.

[12] The Department of Justice delegated to Education in 1991 responsibility for investigating complaints relating to public elementary, secondary, and postsecondary schools under Title II of the Americans with Disabilities Act.

[13] We also found no statistically significant difference between girls and boys with physical disabilities or long-term health problems in the number of days they attend PE class, according to YRBS 2005 estimates.

[14] According to 2006 SHPPS estimates, among schools that required PE, the percentage of schools that have policies allowing students to be exempt from a required PE class for a long-term physical, medical, or cognitive disability increased from the last SHPPS survey in 2000. It is unclear whether changes to exemption policies have impacted the rates of actual exemptions. We found that while many of the districts we visited technically have policies that allowed students with disabilities to be exempted from PE, very few students in the schools we visited were actually exempted.

[15] These estimates have 95 percent confidence intervals within plus or minus 3 percentage points.

[16] SEELS estimates have 95 percent confidence intervals within plus or minus 2 percentage points. NLTS2 estimates have 95 percent confidence intervals within plus or minus 4 percentage points.

[17] Seven percent of students with disabilities between grades 1 and 7 were provided adapted PE services by their school in 2000, according to our estimates of SEELS data; 9 percent of students with disabilities between grades 7 and 12 were provided adapted PE services by their school in 2001, according to our estimates of NLTS2 data. Both of these estimates have 95 percent confidence intervals, within plus or minus 2 percentage points.

[18] Information provided by researchers at Center on Disability Health and Adapted Physical Activity, University of Wisconsin-LaCrosse.

[19] This estimate has a 95 percent confidence interval within plus or minus 2 percentage points.

[20] Out of the 10 districts we visited, 8 could provide us with data on students who take all of their PE in a self-contained, adapted PE class. District officials we interviewed said that some of their students spend part of their time in general PE and part of their time in a separate PE class. Such instances are not included in these percentages.

[21] In elementary school, PE may be taught by a general classroom teacher, while in secondary school, PE may be taught by a PE teacher (with a teacher's license in PE). According to the National Association for Sport and Physical Education in their 2006 Shape of the Nation report, most states require that secondary school teachers who teach PE be certified or licensed by the state in PE (90 percent for high school and 84 percent for middle school/junior high). In contrast, 57 percent of states require this certification at the elementary school level.

[22] This concern is not unique to physical education. Some officials and parents we spoke with noted that teachers' ability to include students with disabilities in the general education classroom is a concern across all subjects. Prior GAO work has shown that teacher preparation programs vary in the extent to which they provide training on instructing

students with disabilities in the general education classroom, and programs face challenges to providing additional training. GAO, *Teacher Preparation: Multiple Federal Education Offices Support Teacher Preparation for Instructing Students with Disabilities and English Language Learners, but Systematic Departmentwide Coordination Could Enhance This Assistance,* GAO-09-573 (Washington, D.C.: July 20, 2009).

[23] This estimate has a 95 percent confidence interval within plus or minus 5 percentage points.

[24] The Elementary and Secondary Education Act of 1965, as amended by the No Child Left Behind Act of 2001. Pub. L. No. 107-110 (2002).

[25] Of the five states we visited, all had PE requirements for students in elementary, middle, and high school, according to state officials and our review of state documents, although specific PE requirements varied.

[26] SEELS and NLTS2 estimates have 95 percent confidence intervals, within plus or minus three percentage points.

[27] Department of Education, Office of Special Education Programs, *SEELS: The Other 80% of Their Time: The Experiences of Elementary and Middle School Students with Disabilities in Their Nonschool Hours* (Washington, D.C., October 2002) and Department of Education, Office of Special Education Programs, *Life Outside the Classroom for Youth with Disabilities: A Report from the National Longitudinal Transition Study-2* (NLST2) (Washington, D.C., April 2003)

[28] In grades 1 through 7, 45 percent of boys with disabilities participated on a school or community-based sports team compared to 31 percent of girls, according to SEELS estimates. In grades 7 through 12, 37 percent of boys with disabilities participated on a school or community-based sports team compared to 23 percent of girls, according to NLTS2 estimates. Differences between genders are statistically significant at the 95 percent confidence level, and estimates have confidence intervals within plus or minus 5 percentage points.

[29] Most states and districts we visited did not regularly track rates of participation in athletics for students with disabilities but district officials were generally able to compile this information based on our request.

[30] These sports teams could be either school-based or community-based. Differences are statistically significant at the 95 percent confidence level.

[31] Special Olympics provides year-round sports training and athletic competition in a variety of Olympic-type sports for children ages 8 and older and adults who qualify. To be eligible, athletes must have an intellectual disability, a cognitive delay, or a development disability. (They may also have a physical disability.) Special Olympics does not exclude any eligible athletes due to qualifying scores. Like Special Olympics, the Paralympics is another international sporting organization that is recognized by the International Olympic Committee. Paralympic athletes are generally those with amputations, cerebral palsy, intellectual disabilities, visual impairments, and spinal injuries. Unlike Special Olympics, the Paralympics is focused on elite performance sport and athletes must go through stringent qualification processes to compete.

[32] Some states' athletic associations or districts have policies that prohibit students older than a certain age (e.g., 19 years old) from playing on school athletic teams.

[33] Florida state athletic officials said they decided to start their adapted athletics program because they received a request from a parent and student.

[34] IDEA specifies that Education's monitoring priorities are (1) the provision of a free appropriate public education in the least restrictive environment, (2) states' exercise of general supervisory authority, and (3) disproportionate representation of racial and ethnic groups in special education and related services. Monitoring of states' exercise of general supervisory authority includes ensuring that states have systems or procedures to identify and correct noncompliance, resolve disputes in a timely manner, and improve educational results and functional outcomes for children with disabilities, according to Education officials and monitoring guidance.

[35] We reviewed additional information from OCR on all of the relevant complaints from the 7 states we interviewed. Of 20 complaints, 14 were focused on extracurricular athletics, one was focused on PE, and two were focused on both PE and extracurricular athletics. The focus of three complaints was unclear based on the information provided. Regarding the outcome of the 20 complaints we reviewed: 11 were administratively closed (complainant withdrew the complaint, no written consent was received, or complaint allegation was currently being investigated elsewhere); 6 were closed due to insufficient evidence of discrimination (including one case in which one allegation was dismissed because it was no longer appropriate for complaint resolution, and there was insufficient factual basis of discrimination concerning the second allegation); and 3 were resolved with a resolution agreement.

[36] For example, OCR issued "Dear Colleague" letters to remind schools, districts, and others of their responsibilities under federal laws and regulations, such as prohibiting the discrimination of students with disabilities who are otherwise qualified to participate in accelerated academic programs or prohibiting discrimination on the basis of sex in education programs or activities. Such letters have highlighted the requirements under federal law and implementing regulations, provided examples of deficiencies or violations, and reminded recipients that OCR enforcement offices are available to answer questions or provide additional technical assistance.

[37] The amount and percentage of the Carol M. White Physical Education Program grants used to serve the specific needs of students with disabilities was provided by OSDFS program officials. Officials said that they provided these by reviewing grant documents, such as applications and annual reports, and grant files and by corresponding directly with grantees. Officials said they did not include grants that indicated that they were serving students with disabilities in their regular PE programs but did not provide services or equipment specifically for students with disabilities.

[38] OSDFS officials who manage the Carol M. White Physical Education Program told us that while they do not currently coordinate with OSEP officials on providing technical assistance to grantees to help them better address the needs of students with disabilities, they plan to do so with the fiscal year 2010 grantee cohort.

[39] Teachers mentioned www.PEcentral.com and www.PElinks4U.org as examples of online resources they use.

[40] Specifically, we reviewed data provided by Education on relevant grants, as well as complaints received by the Office for Civil Rights regarding PE or athletic opportunities for elementary and secondary school students with disabilities under Section 504. Based on interviews with agency officials, we determined these data were sufficiently reliable for the purposes of this report.

[41] See Centers for Disease Control and Prevention, *Fact sheet: SHPPS 2006: Physical Education for Students with Disabilities*; and Sarah M. Lee, Charlene R Burgeson, Janet E. Fulton, and Christine G. Spain, "Physical Education and Physical Activity: Results From the School Health Policies and Programs Study 2006," *The Journal of School Health*, vol. 77, no. 8 (October 2007): 435.

[42] SEELS and NLTS2 used a two-stage process to generate a stratified cluster sample of students receiving special education in a nationally representative sample of local education areas and a sample of state-supported special schools. YRBS used a three-stage stratified cluster sample to produce a representative sample of students in grades 9 through 12.

[43] If independent samples are taken repeatedly from the same population and a confidence interval is calculated for each sample, then a certain percentage of the intervals will include the unknown population measure. The confidence interval is often calculated so that the percentage is 95 percent.

[44] Research Triangle Institute, *SUDAAN: User's Manual, Release 8.0*, vols. 1 and 2 (Research Triangle Park, N.C.: Research Triangle Institute, 2001). SUDAAN® is a registered trademark of the Research Triangle Institute.

[45] We obtained information on states' PE requirements from the 2006 SHPPS of the Department of Health and Human Services' Centers for Disease Control and Prevention.

[46] Socio-economic status was gauged by using percentages of students receiving free or reduced-price lunch.

[47] We contacted a parent center in Florida and met with center staff, but no parents attended our meeting. We met with parents in one parent center in New Jersey. Staff from an additional parent center in New Jersey held an informal discussion with a group of parents to discuss our questions, which GAO staff was unable to attend. Center staff sent us the minutes from that discussion.

Chapter Sources

The following chapters ha ve been previously published:

Chapter 1 – This is an edited reformatted and augmented version of United States Government Accountability Office publication, report GAO-10-812SP, July 2010.

Chapter 2 – This is an edited reformatted and augmented version of a United States Government Accountability Office publication, report GAO-10-519, June 2010.

INDEX

D

E

F

G

H

I

K

L

M

N

O

P

R

S

T

U

V

W